Living Sober

*"...treatment primarily involves
not taking a drink...."*

American Medical Association

Alcoholics Anonymous World Services, Inc., New York

*This is A.A. General Service
Conference-approved literature*

Living Sober
Copyright © 1975; 1998 by
Alcoholics Anonymous World Services, Inc.
475 Riverside Drive, New York, NY 10115
All rights reserved.

Mail address:
Box 459, Grand Central Station, New York, NY 10163

Thirty-first Printing, 1998

Library of Congress Catalog Card No. 75-328153

ISBN 0-916856-04-6

100M - 9/98 (R)   Printed in the U.S.A.

About that title...

Even the words "stay sober"—let alone *live* sober—offended many of us when we first heard such advice. Although we had done a lot of drinking, many of us never felt drunk, and were sure we almost never appeared or sounded drunk. Many of us never staggered, fell, or got thick tongues; many others were never disorderly, never missed a day at work, never had automobile accidents, and certainly were never hospitalized nor jailed for drunkenness.

We knew lots of people who drank more than we did, and people who could not handle their drinks at all. We were not like that. So the suggestion that maybe we should "stay sober" was almost insulting.

Besides, it seemed unnecessarily drastic. How could we live that way? Surely, there was nothing wrong with a cocktail or two at a business lunch or before dinner. Wasn't everyone entitled to relax with a few drinks, or have a couple of beers before going to bed?

However, after we learned some of the facts about the illness called alcoholism, our opinions shifted. Our eyes have been opened to the fact that apparently millions of people have the disease of alcoholism. Medical science does not explain its "cause," but medical experts on alcoholism assure us that any drinking at all leads to trouble for the alcoholic, or problem drinker. Our experience overwhelmingly confirms this.

So not drinking at all—that is, staying sober—becomes the basis of recovery from alcoholism. And let it be emphasized: Living sober turns out to be not at all grim, boring, and uncomfortable, as we had feared, but rather something we begin to enjoy and find much more exciting than our drinking days. We'll show you how.

Some tips on
LIVING SOBER

Some questions often asked by new nondrinkers — and pages that offer some answers

Why 'not drinking'?

We members of Alcoholics Anonymous see the answer to that question when we look honestly at our own past lives. Our experience clearly proves that any drinking at all leads to serious trouble for the alcoholic, or problem drinker. In the words of the American Medical Association:

Alcohol, aside from its addictive qualities, also has a psychological effect that modifies thinking and reasoning. One drink can change the thinking of an alcoholic so that he feels he can tolerate another, and then another, and another. . . .

The alcoholic can learn to completely control his disease, but the affliction cannot be cured so that he can return to alcohol without adverse consequences. *

And we repeat: Somewhat to our surprise, staying sober turns out not to be the grim, wet-blanket experience we had expected! While we were drinking, a life without alcohol seemed like no life at all. But for most members of A.A., living sober is *really* living—a joyous experience. We much prefer it to the troubles we had with drinking.

One more note: anyone can *get* sober. We have all done it lots of times. The trick is to stay and to *live* sober. That is what this booklet is about.

* *From an official statement issued July 31, 1964*

1 Using this booklet

This booklet does *not* offer a plan for recovery from alcoholism. The Alcoholics Anonymous Steps that summarize its program of recovery are set forth in detail in the books "Alcoholics Anonymous" and "Twelve Steps and Twelve Traditions." Those Steps are not interpreted here, nor are the processes they cover discussed in this booklet.

Here, we tell only some methods we have used for living *without* drinking. You are welcome to all of them, whether you are interested in Alcoholics Anonymous or not.

Our drinking was connected with many habits—big and little. Some of them were thinking habits, or things we felt inside ourselves. Others were doing habits—things we did, actions we took.

In getting used to not drinking, we have found that we needed new habits to take the place of those old ones.

(For example, instead of taking that next drink—the one in your hand or the one you've been planning on—can you just postpone it until you read to the bottom of page 6? Sip some soda or fruit juice, instead of an alcoholic beverage, while you read. A little later, we'll explain more fully what's behind this change in habits.)

After we spent a few months practicing these new, sober habits or ways of acting and thinking, they became almost second nature to most of us, as drinking used to be. Not drinking has become natural and easy, not a long, dreary struggle.

These practical, hour-by-hour methods can easily be used at home, at work, or in social gatherings. Also included here are several things we have learned *not* to do, or to avoid. These were things that, we now see, once tempted us to drink or otherwise endangered our recovery.

We think you'll find many or even all of the suggestions discussed here valuable in living sober, with comfort and ease. There is nothing significant about the order in which the booklet presents them. They can be rearranged in any way you like that *works*. Nor is this a complete listing. Practically every A.A. member you meet can give you at least one more good idea not mentioned here. And you will probably come up with brand-new ones that work for you. We hope you pass them on to others who can also profit by them.

A.A. as a fellowship does not formally endorse nor recommend for all alcoholics every line of action included here. But each practice mentioned has proved useful to some members, and may be helpful to you.

This booklet is planned as a handy manual for consulting from time to time, not something to be read straight through just once, then forgotten.

Here are two cautions which have proved helpful:

A. Keep an open mind. Perhaps some of the suggestions offered here will not appeal to you. If that is the case, we have found that, instead of rejecting them forever, it's a better idea to just set them aside for the time being. If we don't close our minds to them permanently, we can always go back later on and try out ideas we didn't like before—if we want to.

For instance, some of us found that, in our initial nondrinking days, the suggestions and comradeship offered by an A.A. sponsor helped us greatly to stay sober. Others of us waited until we had visited many groups and met many A.A.'s before we finally called on a sponsor's help.

Some of us found formal prayer a strong aid in not drinking, while others fled from anything that suggested religion. But all of us are free to change our minds on these ideas later if we choose.

Many of us found that the sooner we started work on the Twelve Steps offered as a program of recovery in the book "Alcoholics Anonymous," the better. Others of us felt the need to postpone this until we had been sober a little while.

The point is, there is no prescribed A.A. "right" way or "wrong" way. Each of us uses what is best for himself or herself—without closing the door on other kinds of help we may find valuable at another time. And each of us tries to respect others' rights to do things differently.

Sometimes, an A.A. member will talk about taking the various parts of the program in cafeteria style—selecting what he likes and letting alone what he does not want. Maybe others will come along and pick up the unwanted parts—or maybe that member himself will go back later and take some of the ideas he previously rejected.

However, it is good to remember the temptation in a cafeteria to pick up nothing but a lot of desserts or starches or salads or some other food we particularly like. It serves as an important reminder to us to keep a balance in our lives.

In recovering from alcoholism, we found that we needed a *balanced* diet of ideas, even if some of them did not look, at first, as enjoyable as others. Like good food, good ideas did us no good unless we made intelligent use of them. And that leads to our second caution.

B. Use your common sense. We found that we have to use plain everyday intelligence in applying the suggestions that follow.

Like almost any other ideas, the suggestions in this booklet can be misused. For example, take the notion of eating candy. Obviously, alcoholics with diabetes, obesity, or blood-sugar problems have had to find substitutes, so they would not endanger their health, yet could still get the benefit of the candy-eating *idea* in recovery from alcoholism. (Many nutritionists favor protein-rich snacks over sweets as a general practice.) Also, it's not good for anybody to overdo this remedy. We should eat balanced meals in addition to the candy.

Another example is the use of the slogan "Easy Does It." Some of us have found that we could abuse this sensible notion, turning it into an excuse for tardiness, laziness, or rudeness. That is not, of course, what the slogan is intended for. Properly applied, it can be healing; misapplied, it can hinder our recovery. Some among us would add to it: "'Easy Does It'—but do it!"

It's clear that we have to use our intelligence in following any advice. Every method described here needs to be used with good judgment.

One more thing. A.A. does not pretend to offer scientific expertise on staying sober. We can share with you only our own personal experience, not professional theories and explanations.

So these pages offer no new medical shortcuts on how to stop drinking if you are still doing it, nor any miraculous secrets for shortening or avoiding a hangover.

Sometimes, getting sober can be done on your own at home; but frequently, prolonged drinking has caused such serious medical problems that you would be better advised to seek medical or hospital help for drying out. If you are that seriously ill, you may need such professional services before you can possibly be interested in what we offer here.

Many of us who were not that sick, however, have sweated it out in the company of other A.A. members. Because we have been through it ourselves, we can often help—in a layman's way—to relieve some of the misery and suffering. At least, we understand. We have been there.

So this booklet is about *not* drinking (rather than about *stopping* drinking). It's about living sober.

We have found that for us recovery *began* with not drinking—with getting sober and staying completely free of alcohol in any amount, and in any form. We have also found that we have to stay away from other mind-changing drugs. We can move toward a full and satisfying life only when we stay sober. Sobriety is the launching pad for our recovery.

In a way, this booklet is about how to handle sobriety. (Before, we couldn't; so we drank.)

2 Staying away from the first drink

Expressions commonly heard in A.A. are "If you don't take that first drink, you can't get drunk" and "One drink is too many, but twenty are not enough."

Many of us, when we first began to drink, never wanted or took more than one or two drinks. But as time went on, we increased the number. Then, in later years, we found ourselves drinking more and more, some of us getting and staying very drunk. Maybe our condition didn't always show in our speech or our gait, but by this time we were never actually sober.

If that bothered us too much, we would cut down, or try to limit ourselves to just one or two, or switch from hard liquor to beer or wine. At least, we tried to limit the amount, so we would not get too disastrously tight. Or we tried to hide how much we drank.

But all these measures got more and more difficult. Occasionally, we even went on the wagon, and did not drink at all for a while.

Eventually, we would go back to drinking—just one drink. And since that apparently did no serious damage, we felt it was safe to have another. Maybe that was all we took on that occasion, and it was a great relief to find we could take just one or two, then stop. Some of us did that many times.

But the experience proved to be a snare. It persuaded us that we could drink safely. And then there would come the occasion (some special celebration, a personal loss, or no particular event at all) when two or three made us feel fine, so we thought one or two more could not hurt. And with absolutely no intention of doing so, we found ourselves again drinking too much. We were right back where we had been—overdrinking without really wanting to.

Such repeated experiences have forced us to this logically inescapable conclusion: If we do not take the first drink, we never get drunk. Therefore, instead of planning never to get drunk, or trying to limit the number of drinks or the amount of alcohol, we have learned to concentrate on avoiding only one drink: the first one.

In effect, instead of worrying about limiting the number of drinks at the end of a drinking episode, we avoid the one drink that starts it.

Sounds almost foolishly simplistic, doesn't it? It's hard for many of us now to believe that we never really figured this out for ourselves before we came to A.A. (Of course, to tell the truth, we never really wanted to give up drinking altogether, either, until we learned about alcoholism.) But the main point is: We know now that this is what works.

Instead of trying to figure out how many we could handle—four?—six?—a dozen?—we remember, "Just don't pick up that first drink." It is so much simpler. The habit of thinking this way has helped hundreds of thousands of us stay sober for years.

Doctors who are experts on alcoholism tell us that there is a sound medical foundation for avoiding the first drink. It is the first drink which triggers, immediately or some time later, the compulsion to drink more and more until we are in drinking trouble again. Many of us have come to believe that our alcoholism is an addiction to the drug alcohol; like addicts of any sort who want to maintain recovery, we have to keep away from the first dose of the drug we have become addicted to. Our experience seems to prove this, as you can read in the book "Alcoholics Anonymous" and in our Grapevine magazine, and as you can hear wherever A.A. members get together and share their experiences.

3 Using the 24-hour plan

In our drinking days, we often had such bad times that we swore, "Never again." We took pledges for as long as a year, or promised someone we would not touch the stuff for three weeks, or three months. And of course, we tried going on the wagon for various periods of time.

We were absolutely sincere when we voiced these declarations through gritted teeth. With all our hearts, we wanted never to be drunk again. We were determined. We swore off drinking altogether, intending to stay off alcohol well into some indefinite future.

Yet, in spite of our intentions, the outcome was almost inevitably the same. Eventually, the memory of the vows, and of the suffering that led to them, faded. We drank again, and we wound up in more trouble. Our dry "forever" had not lasted very long.

Some of us who took such pledges had a private reservation: We told ourselves that the promise not to drink applied only to "hard stuff," not to beer or wine. In that way we learned, if we did not already know it, that beer and wine could get us drunk, too—we just had to drink more of them to get the same effects we got on distilled spirits. We wound up as stoned on beer or wine as we had been before on the hard stuff.

Yes, others of us did give up alcohol completely and did keep our pledges exactly as promised, until the time was up…. Then we ended the drought by drinking again, and were soon right back in trouble, with an additional load of new guilt and remorse.

With such struggles behind us now, in A.A. we try to avoid the expressions "on the wagon" and "taking the pledge." They remind us of our failures.

Although we realize that alcoholism is a permanent, irreversible condition, our experience has taught us to make no long-term promises about staying sober. We have found it more realistic—and more successful—to say, "I am not taking a drink *just for today.*"

Even if we drank yesterday, we can plan not to drink today. We may drink tomorrow—who knows whether we'll even be alive then?—but for *this* 24 hours, we decide not to drink. No matter what the temptation or provocation, we determine to go to any extremes necessary to avoid a drink *today.*

Our friends and families are understandably weary of hearing us vow, "This time I really mean it," only to see us lurch home loaded. So we do not promise them, or even each other, not to drink. Each of us promises only herself or himself. It is, after all, our own health and life at stake. We, not our family or friends, have to take the necessary steps to stay well.

If the desire to drink is really strong, many of us chop the 24 hours down into smaller parts. We decide not to drink for, say, at least one hour. We can endure the temporary discomfort of not drinking for just one more hour; then one more, and so on. Many of us began our recovery in just this way. In fact, *every recovery from alcoholism began with one sober hour.*

One version of this is simply postponing the (next) drink.

(How about it? Still sipping soda? Have you really postponed that drink we mentioned back on page 1? If so, this can be the beginning of your recovery.)

The next drink will be available later, but right now, we postpone taking it at least for the present day, or moment. (Say, for the rest of this page?)

The 24-hour plan is very flexible. We can start it afresh at any time, wherever we are. At home, at work, in a bar or in a hospital room, at 4:00 p.m. or at 3:00 a.m., we can decide right then not to take a drink during the forthcoming 24 hours, or five minutes.

Continually renewed, this plan avoids the weakness of such methods as going on the wagon or taking a pledge. A period on the wagon and a pledge both eventually came, as planned, to an end—so we felt free to drink again. But today is always here. Life *is* daily; today is all we have; and anybody can go one day without drinking.

First, we try living in the now just in order to stay sober—and it works. Once the idea has become a part of our thinking, we find that living life in 24-hour segments is an effective and satisfying way to handle many other matters as well.

4 Remembering that alcoholism is an incurable, progressive, fatal disease

Many people in the world know they cannot eat certain foods—oysters or strawberries or eggs or cucumbers or sugar or something else—without getting very uncomfortable and maybe even quite sick.

A person with a food allergy of this kind can go around feeling a lot of self-pity, complaining to everyone that he or she is unfairly deprived, and constantly whining about not being able, or allowed, to eat something delicious.

Obviously, even though we may feel cheated, it isn't wise to ignore our own physiological makeup. If our limitations are ignored, severe discomfort or illness may result. To stay healthy and reasonably happy, we must learn to live with the bodies we have.

One of the new thinking habits a recovering alcoholic can develop is a calm view of himself or herself as someone who needs to avoid chemicals (alcohol and other drugs that are substitutes for it) if he or she wants to maintain good health.

We have as evidence our own drinking days, a total of hundreds of thousands of man- or woman-years of a whale of a lot of drinking. We know that, as the drinking years went by, our problems related to drinking continually worsened. Alcoholism is progressive.

Oh, of course, many of us had periods when, for some months or even years, we sometimes thought the drinking had sort of straightened itself out. We seemed able to maintain a pretty heavy alcohol intake fairly safely. Or we would stay sober except for occasional drunk nights, and the drinking was not getting noticeably worse, as far as we could see. Nothing horrible or dramatic happened.

However, we can now see that, in the long or short haul, our drinking problem inevitably got more serious.

Some physicians expert on alcoholism tell us there is no doubt that alcoholism steadily grows worse as one grows older. (Know anyone who *isn't* growing older?)

We are also convinced, after the countless attempts we made to prove otherwise, that alcoholism is incurable—just like some other illnesses. It cannot be "cured" in this sense: We cannot change our body chemistry and go back to being the normal, moderate social drinkers lots of us seemed to be in our youth.

As some of us put it, we can no more make that change than a pickle can change itself back into a cucumber. No medication or psychological treatment any of us ever had "cured" our alcoholism.

Further, having seen thousands and thousands of alcoholics who did *not* stop drinking, we are strongly persuaded that alcoholism is a fatal disease. Not only have we seen many alcoholics drink themselves to death—dying during the "withdrawal" symptoms of delirium tremens (D.T.'s) or convulsions, or dying of cirrhosis of the liver directly related to drinking—we also know that many deaths not officially attributed to alcoholism are in reality caused by it. Often, when an automobile accident, drowning, suicide, homicide, heart attack, fire, pneumonia, or stroke is listed as the immediate cause of death, it was heavy alcoholic drinking that led to the fatal condition or event.

Certainly, most of us in A.A. felt safely far away from such a fate when we were drinking. And probably the majority of us never came near the horrible last stages of chronic alcoholism.

But we saw that we *could,* if we just kept on drinking. If you get on a bus bound for a town a thousand miles away, that's where you'll wind up, unless you get off and move in another direction.

Okay. What do you do if you learn that you have an incurable, progressive, fatal disease—whether it's alcoholism or some other, such as a heart condition or cancer?

Many people just deny it is true, ignore the condition, accept no treatment for it, suffer, and die.

But there is another way.

You can accept the "diagnosis"—persuaded by your doctor, your friends, or yourself. Then you can find out what can be done, if anything, to keep the condition "under control," so you can still live many happy, productive, healthy years *as long as you take proper care of yourself.* You recognize fully the seriousness of your condition, and you do the sensible things necessary to carry on a healthy life.

This, it turns out, is surprisingly easy in regard to alcoholism, if you really want to stay well. And since we A.A.'s have learned to enjoy life so much, we really want to stay well.

We try never to lose sight of the unchangeable fact of our alcoholism, but we learn not to brood or feel sorry for ourselves or talk about it all the time. We accept it as a characteristic of our body—like our height or our need for glasses, or like any allergies we may have.

Then we can figure out how to live comfortably—not bitterly—with that knowledge as long as we start out by simply avoiding that *first* drink (remember?) just for today.

A blind member of A.A. said his alcoholism was quite similar to his blindness. "Once I accepted the loss of my sight," he explained, "and took the rehabilitation training available to me, I discovered I really can, with the aid of my cane or my dog, go anywhere I want to go quite safely, just as long as I don't forget or ignore the fact that I am blind. But when I do not act within the knowledge that I cannot see, it is then I get hurt, or in trouble."

"If you want to get well," one A.A. woman said, "you just take your treatment and follow directions and go on living. It's easy as long as you remember the new facts about your health. Who has time to feel 'deprived' or self-pitying when you find there are so many delights connected with living happily unafraid of your illness?"

To summarize: We remember we have an incurable, potentially fatal ailment called alcoholism. And instead of persisting in drinking, we prefer to figure out, and use, enjoyable ways of living without alcohol.

We need not be ashamed that we have a disease. It is no disgrace. No one knows exactly why some people become alcoholics while others don't. It is not our fault. We did not *want* to become alcoholics. We did not *try* to get this illness.

We did not suffer alcoholism just because we enjoyed it, after all. We did not deliberately, maliciously set out to do the things we were later ashamed of. We did them against our better judgment and instinct because we were really sick, and didn't even know it.

We've learned that no good comes of useless regret and worry about how we got this way. The first step toward feeling better, and getting over our sickness, is quite simply not drinking.

Try the idea on for size. Wouldn't you rather recognize you have a health condition which can be successfully treated, than spend a lot of time miserably worrying about what's wrong with you? We have found this is a better-looking, and better-feeling, picture of ourselves than the old gloomy selves we used to see. It is truer, too. We know. The proof of it is in the way we feel, act, and think—now.

Anyone who wants it is welcome to a "free trial period" of this new concept of self. Afterward, anyone who wants the old days again is perfectly free to start them all over. It is your right to take back your misery if you want it.

On the other hand, you can also keep the new picture of yourself, if you'd rather. It, too, is yours by right.

5 'Live and Let Live'

The old saying "Live and Let Live" seems so commonplace, it is easy to overlook its value. Of course, one reason it has been said over and over for years is that it has proved beneficial in so many ways.

We A.A.'s make some special uses of it to help us not drink. It particularly helps us cope with people who get on our nerves.

Reviewing once more a little of our drinking histories, many of us can see how very, very often our drinking problem appeared to be related somehow to other people. Experimenting with beer or wine in our teen-age years seemed natural, since so many others were doing it, and we wanted their approval. Then came weddings and bar mitzvahs and christenings and holidays and football games and cocktail parties and business lunches...and the list can go on and on. In all of these circumstances, we drank at least partly because everybody else was drinking and seemed to expect us to.

Those of us who began to drink alone, or to sneak a drink now and then, often did so to keep some other person or people from knowing how much, or how often, we drank. We rarely liked to hear anybody else talk about our drinking. If they did, we frequently told them "reasons" for our drinking, as if we wanted to ward off criticism or complaints.

Some of us found ourselves argumentative or even belligerent toward other people after drinking. Yet others of us felt we really got along better with people after a drink or two—whether it was a social evening, a tense sale or job interview, or even making love.

Our drinking caused many of us to choose our friends according to how much they drank. We even changed friends when we felt we had "outgrown" their drinking styles. We preferred "real drinkers" to people who just took one or two. And we tried to avoid teetotalers.

Many of us were guilty and angry about the way our family reacted to our drinking. Some of us lost jobs because a boss or a colleague at work objected to our drinking. We wished people would mind their own business and leave us alone!

Often, we felt angry and fearful even toward people who had not criticized us. Our guilt made us extra sensitive to those around us, and we nursed grudges. Sometimes, we changed bars, changed jobs, or moved to new neighborhoods just to get away from certain persons.

So a great number of people besides ourselves were in one way or another involved in our drinking, to some degree.

When we first stopped drinking, it was a great relief to find that the people we met in A.A.—recovered alcoholics—seemed to be quite different. They reacted to us, not with criticism and suspicion, but with understanding and concern.

However, it is perfectly natural that we still encounter some people who get on our nerves, both within A.A. and outside it. We may find that our non-A.A. friends, co-workers, or family members still treat us as if we were drinking. (It may take them a little while to believe that we have *really* stopped. After all, they may have seen us stop many times in the past, only to start again.)

To begin to put the concept of "Live and Let Live" into practice, we must face this fact: There *are* people in A.A., and everywhere else, who sometimes say things we disagree with, or do things we don't like. Learning to live with differences is essential to our comfort. It is exactly in those cases that we have found it extremely helpful to say to ourselves, "Oh, well, 'Live and Let Live.'"

In fact, in A.A. much emphasis is placed on learning how to tolerate other people's behavior. However offensive or distasteful it may seem to us, it is certainly *not* worth drinking about. Our own recovery is too important. Alcoholism can and does kill, we recall.

We have learned it pays to make a very special effort to try to understand other people, especially anyone who rubs us the wrong way. For our recovery, it is more important to understand than to be understood. This is not very difficult if we bear in mind that the other A.A. members, too, are trying to understand, just as we are.

For that matter, we'll meet some people in A.A. or elsewhere who won't be exactly crazy about us, either. So all of us try to respect the rights of others to act as they choose (or must). We can then expect them to give us the same courtesy. In A.A., they generally do.

Usually, people who like each other—in a neighborhood, a company, a club, or A.A.—gravitate toward each other. When we spend time with people we like, we are less annoyed by those we don't particularly care for.

As time goes on, we find we are not afraid simply to walk away from people who irritate us, instead of meekly letting them get under our skin, or instead of trying to straighten them out just so they will suit us better.

None of us can remember anyone's forcing us to drink alcohol. No one ever tied us down and poured booze down our gullets. Just as no one *physically* compelled us to drink, now we try to make sure no one will *mentally* "drive us to drink," either.

It is very easy to use other people's actions as an alibi for drinking. We used to be experts at it. But in sobriety, we have learned a new technique: We never let ourselves get so resentful toward someone else that we allow that person to control our lives—especially to the extent of causing us to drink. We have found we have no desire to let any other person run, or ruin, our lives.

An ancient sage said that none of us should criticize another until we have walked a mile in the other person's boots. This wise advice can give us greater compassion for our fellow human beings. And putting it into practice makes us feel much better than being hung-over.

"Let Live"—yes. But some of us find just as much value in the first part of the slogan: "Live"!

When we have worked out ways to enjoy *our own* living fully, then we are content to let other people live any way they want. If our own lives are interesting and productive, we really have no impulse or desire to find fault with others or worry about the way they act.

Can you think right this minute of someone who really bothers you?

If you can, try something. Postpone thinking about him or her and whatever it is about the person that riles you. You can boil inside about it later if you want to. But for right now, why not put it off while you read the next paragraph?

Live! Be concerned with your own living. In our opinion, staying sober opens up the way to life and happiness. It is worth sacrificing many a grudge or argument. . . . Okay, so you didn't manage to keep your mind completely off that other person. Let's see whether the suggestion coming next will help.

6 Getting active

It is very hard just to sit still trying *not* to do a certain thing, or *not* even to think about it. It's much easier to get active and do something *else*—other than the act we're trying to avoid.

So it is with drinking. Simply trying to avoid a drink (or not think of one), all by itself, doesn't seem to be enough. The more we think about the drink we're trying to keep away from, the more it occupies our mind, of course. And that's no good. It's better to get busy with something, almost anything, that will use our mind and channel our energy toward health.

Thousands of us wondered what we would do, once we stopped drinking, with all that time on our hands. Sure enough, when we did stop, all those hours we had once spent planning, getting our drinks, drinking, and recovering from its immediate effects, suddenly turned into big, empty holes of time that had to be filled somehow.

Most of us had jobs to do. But even so, there were some pretty long, vacant stretches of minutes and hours staring at us. We needed new habits of activity to fill those open spaces and utilize the nervous energy previously absorbed by our preoccupation, or our obsession, with drinking.

Anyone who has ever tried to break a habit knows that substituting a new and different activity is easier than just stopping the old activity and putting nothing in its place.

Recovered alcoholics often say, "Just stopping drinking is not enough." Just *not drinking* is a negative, sterile thing. That is clearly demonstrated by our experience. To *stay* stopped, we've found we need to put in place of the drinking a positive program of action. We've had to learn how to *live* sober.

Fear may have originally pushed some of us toward looking into the possibility that we might have a drinking problem. And over a short period, fear alone may help some of us stay away from a drink. But a fearful state is not a very happy or relaxed one to maintain for very long. So we try to develop a healthy respect for the power of alcohol, instead of a fear of it, just as people have a healthy respect for cyanide, iodine, or any other poison. Without going around in constant fear of those potions, most people respect what they can do to the body, and have enough sense not to imbibe them. We in A.A. now have the same knowledge of, and regard for, alcohol. But, of course, it is based on firsthand experience, not on seeing a skull and crossbones on a label.

We can't rely on fear to get us through those empty hours without a drink, so what *can* we do?

We have found many kinds of activity useful and profitable, some more than others. Here are two kinds, in the order of their effectiveness as we experienced it.

A. Activity in and around A.A.

When experienced A.A. members say that they found "getting active" helpful in their recovery from alcoholism, they usually mean getting active in and around A.A.

If you want to, you can do that even before you decide whether or not you want to become an A.A. member. You don't need anyone's permission or invitation.

In fact, before you make any decision about a drinking problem, it might be a good idea to spend some time around A.A. Don't worry—just sitting at, and observing, A.A. meetings does not make you an alcoholic or an A.A. member, any more than sitting in a hen house makes you a hen. You can try a sort of "dry run" or "dress rehearsal" of A.A. first, then decide about "joining."

The activities we often use at first in A.A. may seem fairly unimportant, but the results prove them valuable. We might call these things "ice breakers," because they make it easier to feel comfortable around people we do not know.

As most A.A. meetings end, you'll generally notice that some of those present start putting away the folding chairs, or emptying ashtrays, or carrying empty tea and coffee cups to the kitchen.

Join in. You may be surprised at the effect on yourself of such seemingly little chores. You can help wash out the cups and coffeepot, put away the literature, and sweep the floor.

Helping out with these easy little physical tasks does *not* mean you become the group's janitor or custodian. Nothing of the sort. From years of doing it and seeing fellow members do it, we know that practically every person happily recovered in A.A. has taken his or her turn at the K.P. or refreshment-and-cleanup detail. The results we have felt from doing these tasks are concrete, beneficial, and usually surprising.

In fact, many of us began to feel comfortable around A.A. only when we began to help with these simple acts. And we were even more at ease, and much further away from drinking or the thought of it, when we accepted some small, but specific, regular responsibility—such as bringing the refreshments, helping to prepare and serve them, being a greeter on the hospitality committee, or performing other tasks that needed doing. Simply by watching other people, you'll learn what needs to be done to get ready for the A.A. meeting, and to straighten up afterwards.

No one *has* to do such things, of course. In A.A., no one is ever required to do, or not do, anything. But these simple, menial chores and the commitment (only to ourselves) to do them faithfully have had unexpectedly good effects on many of us, and still do. They help give some muscle to our sobriety.

As you stay around an A.A. group, you'll observe other tasks that need undertaking. You'll hear the secretary make announcements and see the treasurer take charge of the contributions basket. Serving in one of those capacities, once you get a little accumulation of nondrinking time (about 90 days, in most groups), is a good way to fill some of the time we used to spend drinking.

When these "jobs" interest you, leaf through a copy of the pamphlet "The A.A. Group." It explains what the group "officers" do, and how they are chosen.

In A.A., no one is "above" or "below" anyone else. There are no classes or strata or hierarchies among the members. There are no formal officers with any governing power or authority whatsoever. A.A. is not an organization in the usual sense of that word. Instead, it is a fellowship of equals. Everybody calls everybody else by first name. A.A.'s take turns doing the services needed for group meetings and other functions.

No particular professional skill or education is needed. Even if you have never been a joiner, or a chairman or secretary of anything, you may find—as most of us have—that within the A.A. group, these services are easy to do, and they do wonders for us. They build a sturdy backbone for our recovery.

Now for the second type of activity that helps keep us away from drinking.

B. Activity not related to A.A.

It's curious, but true, that some of us, when we first stop drinking, seem to experience a sort of temporary failure of the imagination.

It's curious, because during our drinking days, so many of us displayed almost unbelievably fertile powers of imagination. In less than a week, we could dream up instantly more reasons (excuses?) for drinking than most people use for all other purposes in a lifetime. (Incidentally, it's a pretty good rule of thumb that normal drinkers—that is, nonalcoholics—*never* need or use any particular justification for either drinking or not drinking!)

When the need to give ourselves reasons for our drinking is no longer there, it often seems that our minds go on a sit-down strike. Some of us find we can't think up nondrinking things to do! Perhaps this is because we're just out of the habit. Or perhaps the mind needs a period of restful convalescence after active alcoholism ceases. In either case, the dullness does go away. After our first month's sobriety, many of us notice a distinct difference. After three months, our minds seem still clearer. And during our second year of recovery, the change is striking. More mental energy seems available to us than ever before.

But it's during the seemingly endless first dry stretch that you will hear some of us say, "What's to do?"

The following list is just a starter for use at that time. It isn't very thrilling or adventurous, but it covers the kinds of activity many of us have used to fill our first vacant hours when we were not at our jobs or with other nondrinking people. We know they work. We did such things as:

1. *Taking walks*—especially to new places, and in parks or the country. Leisurely, easy strolls, not tiring marches.

2. *Reading*—although some of us got pretty fidgety if we tried to read anything that demanded much concentration.

3. *Going to museums and art galleries.*

4. *Exercising*—swimming, golfing, jogging, yoga, or other forms of exercise your doctor advises.

5. *Starting on long-neglected chores*—cleaning out a bureau drawer, sorting papers, answering a few letters, hanging pictures, or something of the sort that we've been postponing.

We have found it is important, though, *not to overdo* any of these. Planning to clean out all the closets (or the whole attic or garage or basement or apartment) sounds simple. However, after a day's hard physical labor at it, we can wind up exhausted, dirty, not finished, and discouraged. So our advice to each other is: Cut down the plan to a manageable size. Start out, not to straighten up the kitchen or clean out those files, but simply to clean out one drawer or one folder. Do another one another day.

6. *Trying a new hobby*—nothing expensive or very demanding, just

some pleasant, idle diversion in which we do not need to excel or win, but only to enjoy some refreshingly different moments. Many of us have picked up hobbies we'd never dreamed of before, such as bridge, macrame, the opera, tropical fish, cabinetmaking, needlework, baseball, writing, singing, crossword puzzles, cooking, bird-watching, amateur acting, leathercraft, gardening, sailing, the guitar, movies, dancing, marbles, bonsai, collecting something or other. Many of us have found we now really enjoy things that we wouldn't even consider before.

7. Revisiting an old pastime, except you-know-what. Maybe, stored away somewhere, there is a watercolor set you haven't touched in years, a crewel kit, an accordion, table tennis or backgammon equipment, a tape collection, or notes for a novel. For some of us, it has been rewarding to dig these out, dust them off, and try having a go at them again. If you decide they're not for you any more, get rid of them.

8. Taking a course. Have you always wished you could speak Swahili or Russian? Enjoy history or math? Understand archaeology or anthropology? Correspondence courses, instruction on public television, or adult classes (for pleasure, not necessarily for credit) that meet about once a week are usually available somewhere. Why not give one a try? Many of us have found that such a course can not only add a fresh dimension to life, but also lead to a whole new career.

If studying gets to be a drag, though, don't hesitate to drop it. You have the right to change your mind and quit anything that is more of a hassle than it's worth. Being "a quitter" can take courage and make very good sense if we're quitting something that is not good for us, or adds no positive, pleasurable, or healthy new facet to our life.

9. Volunteering to do some useful service. Many, many hospitals, children's agencies, churches, and other institutions and organizations desperately need volunteers for all kinds of activity. The choice is wide, from reading to the blind to sealing envelopes for a church mailing or gathering signatures on a political petition. Check with any nearby hospital, church, governmental agency, or civic club to find out what volunteer services are needed in your community. We've found we feel much better about ourselves when we contribute even a small service for the benefit of our fellow human beings. Even the act of investigating the possibilities of such service is in itself informative and interesting.

10. Doing something about your personal appearance. Most of us let ourselves go pretty much. A new haircut, some new clothes, new glasses, or even new teeth have a marvelously cheering effect. Often, we had been intending to get around to something like that, and the months when we first started staying sober seemed a good time to look into it.

11. Taking a fling at something frivolous! Not everything we do has to be an earnest effort at self-improvement, although any such effort is worthwhile and gives a lift to our self-esteem. Many of us find it important to balance serious periods with things we do for pure fun. Do you like balloons? Zoos? Bubble gum? Marx Brothers movies? Soul music? Reading sci-fi or detective stories? Sunbathing? Snowmobiling? If not, find something else nonalcoholic that rewards you with nothing but sheer enjoyment, and have some "dry" fun. You deserve it.

12. _____

Fill this one in for yourself. Let's hope the list above sparked an idea for you which is different from all of those listed.... It did? Good! Go to it.

One word of caution, though. Some of us find we have a tendency to go overboard, and try too many things at once. We have a good brake for that, which you'll read about on page 44. It's called "Easy Does It."

7 Using the Serenity Prayer

On the walls of thousands of A.A. meeting rooms, in any of a variety of languages, this invocation can be seen:

> God grant us the serenity to accept
> the things we cannot change,
> The courage to change the things we can,
> And the wisdom to know the difference.

A.A. did not originate it. Versions of it seem to have been used for centuries in various faiths, and it is now widely current outside A.A., as well as within the Fellowship. Whether we belong to this church or that, whether we are humanists, agnostics, or atheists, most of us have found these words a wonderful guide in getting sober, staying sober, and enjoying our sobriety. Whether we see the Serenity Prayer as an actual prayer or just as a fervent wish, it offers a simple prescription for a healthy emotional life.

We've put one thing right at the head of the list among "the things we cannot change": our alcoholism. No matter what we do, we know that tomorrow we won't suddenly be nonalcoholic—any more than we'll be ten years younger or six inches taller.

We couldn't change our alcoholism. But we didn't say meekly, "All right, I'm an alcoholic. Guess I'll just have to drink myself to death." There was something we *could* change. We didn't have to be drunk alcoholics. We could become sober alcoholics. Yes, that did take *courage*. And we needed a flash of *wisdom* to see that it was possible, that we could change ourselves.

For us, that was only the first, most obvious use for the Serenity Prayer. The further away we get from the last drink, the more beautiful and the more packed with meaning these few lines become. We can apply them to everyday situations, the kind we used to run away from, into the bottle.

By way of example: "I hate this job. Do I have to stick with it, or can I quit?" A little wisdom comes into play: "Well, if I do quit, the next few weeks or months may be rough, but if I have the guts to take it—'the courage to change'—I think I'll wind up in a better spot."

Or the answer may be: "Let's face it—this is no time for me to go job-hunting, not with a family to support. Besides, here I am six weeks sober, and my A.A. friends say I'd better not start making any drastic changes in my life just yet—better concentrate on not taking that first drink, and wait till I get my head straightened out. Okay, I can't change the job right now. But maybe I can change my own attitude. Let's see. How can I learn to accept the job serenely?"

That word "serenity" looked like an impossible goal when we first saw the prayer. In fact, if serenity meant apathy, bitter resignation, or stolid endurance, then we didn't even want to aim at it. But we found that serenity meant no such thing. When it comes to us now, it is more as plain recognition—a clear-eyed, realistic way of seeing the world, accompanied by inner peace and strength. Serenity is like a gyroscope that lets us keep our balance no matter what turbulence swirls around us. And that *is* a state of mind worth aiming for.

8 Changing old routines

Certain set times, familiar places, and regular activities associated with drinking have been woven closely into the fabric of our lives. Like fatigue, hunger, loneliness, anger, and overelation, these old routines can prove to be traps dangerous to our sobriety.

When we first stopped drinking, many of us found it useful to look back at the habits surrounding our drinking and, whenever possible, to change a lot of the small things connected with drinking.

To illustrate: Many who used to begin the day with an eye-opener in the bathroom now head for coffee in the kitchen. Some of us shifted the order of things we did to prepare for the day, such as eating before bathing and dressing, or vice versa. A change in brands of toothpaste and mouthwash (be careful about the alcohol content!) gave us a fresh, different taste to start out with. We tried a little exercise or a few quiet moments of contemplation or meditation before plunging into the day.

Many of us also learned to try a new route when we first left the house in the morning, *not* passing by a familiar watering hole. Some have switched from the car to a train, from the subway to a bicycle, from a bus to walking. Others joined a different car pool.

Whether our drinking was in the commuter bar car, the neighborhood gin mill, the kitchen, the country club, or the garage, each of us can spot pretty exactly his or her own favorite drinking locale. Whether we were the occasional bender-thrower or the round-the-clock winesipper, each of us knows for himself or herself what days, hours, and occasions have most often been associated with our tippling.

When you want not to drink, it helps to shake up *all* those routines and change the pieces around, we have found. Housewives, for instance, say it helps to shift shopping times and places and rearrange the agenda of daily chores. Working people who used to sneak out for a snort on the coffee break now stay in and really have coffee or tea and a bun. (And that's a good time to call someone you know who's also off the sauce. During times when we used to drink, it's reassuring to talk to a person who has been through the same experiences.)

Those of us who began our sobriety while confined to a hospital or a jail tried to change our daily paths so we would not encounter the institution's bootlegger so often.

For some of us, lunchtime was usually an hour or two of liquid refreshment. When we first stop drinking, instead of going to the restaurant or steak pit where the waiters or the bartender always knew what we wanted without being told, it makes good sense to head in a different direction for lunch, and it's especially helpful to eat with other nondrinkers. "Testing your willpower," in a matter involving health, seems pretty silly when it is not necessary. Instead, we try to make our new health habits as easy as possible.

For many of us, this has also meant forgoing, at least for a while, the company of our hard-drinking buddies. If they are true friends, they naturally are glad to see us take care of our health, and they respect our right to do whatever we want to do, just as we respect their right to drink if they choose. But we have learned to be wary of anyone who persists in urging us to drink again. Those who really love us, it seems, encourage our efforts to stay well.

At 5:00 p.m., or whenever the day's work is done, some of us learned to stop at a sandwich shop for a bite. Then we would take an unfamiliar route for walking home, one that did not lead past our old drinking haunts. If we were commuters, we did not ride in the bar car, and we got off the train at the other end—not near the friendly neighborhood tavern.

When we got home, instead of bringing out the ice cubes and glasses, we changed clothes, then brewed a pot of tea or took some fruit or vegetable juice, took a nap, or relaxed awhile in the shower or with a book or the newspaper. We learned to vary our diet to include foods not closely associated with alcohol. If imbibing and watching TV was our usual after-dinner routine, we found it helped to shift to another room and other activities. If we used to wait for the family to get to bed before hauling out the bottle, we tried going to bed earlier for a change, or taking a walk or reading or writing or playing chess.

Business trips, weekends and holidays, the golf course, baseball and football stadiums, card games, the old swimming pool, or the ski lodge often meant drinking for many of us. Boat people often spent summer days drinking on the bay or the lake. When we first stopped drinking, we found it paid to plan a different kind of trip or holiday for a while. Trying to avoid taking a drink on a vessel loaded with beer drinkers, Tom Collins sippers, flask nippers, sangria lovers, or hot-buttered-rum guzzlers is much harder than simply going to other places and, for novelty's sake, doing new things that do not particularly remind us of drinking.

Suppose we were invited to the kind of cocktail party where the chief entertainment—or business—was drinking. What then? While drinking, we had been pretty skillful at dreaming up alibis, so we just applied that skill to devising a graceful way of saying, "No, thank you." (For parties we really have to attend, we've worked out safe new routines, which are explained on page 65.)

In our early days of not drinking, did we get rid of all the booze around our homes? Yes and no.

Most successful nondrinkers agree that it is a sound precaution at first to get rid of whatever hidden stashes there may be—if we can find them. But opinions vary with regard to the bottles in the liquor cabinet or the wine rack.

Some of us insist that it was never the availability of the beverage that led us to drink, any more than the immediate *un*availability kept us from that drink we really wanted. So some ask: Why pour good Scotch down the drain or even give it away? We live in a drinking society, they say, and cannot avoid the presence of alcoholic beverages forever. Keep the supply on hand to serve when guests arrive, they suggest, and just learn to ignore it the rest of the time. For them, that worked.

A multitude of others among us point out that sometimes it was incredibly easy for us to take a drink on impulse, almost unconsciously, before we intended to. If no alcohol is handy, if we'd have to go out and buy it, we at least have a chance to recognize what we're about to do and can choose *not* to drink instead. Nondrinkers of this persuasion say they found it wiser to be safe than sorry! So they gave away their whole stock and kept none on the premises until their sobriety seemed to be in a fairly steady, stabilized state. Even now, they buy only enough for one evening's guests.

So take your pick. *You* know what your own drinking pattern has been and how you feel about sobriety today.

Now, most of the little changes in routine mentioned in this section may seem, by themselves, ridiculously trivial. However, we can assure you that the sum total of all such alterations in pattern has given many of us an astonishingly powerful propulsion toward newly vigorous health. You can have such a boost, too, if you want it.

9 Eating or drinking something—usually, sweet

Can you imagine drinking a bourbon and soda right after a chocolate malted? Or a beer on top of a piece of cake with icing?

If you're not too ill to read on, you will agree that they don't sound exactly made for each other.

In one way, that is what this portion of our experience is about. Many of us have learned that something sweet-tasting, or almost any nourishing food or snack, seems to dampen a bit the desire for a drink. So, from time to time, we remind each other never to get too hungry.

Maybe it's just imagination, but the yen for a shot does seem to be sharper when the stomach is empty. At least, it's more noticeable.

This booklet is based on our own personal experience, rather than on scientific reports. So we cannot explain precisely, in technical terms, why this should be so. We can only pass on the word that thousands of us—even many who said they had never liked sweets—have found that eating or drinking something sweet allays the urge to drink.

Since we are neither physicians nor nutrition experts, we cannot recommend that everybody carry a chocolate bar and nibble on it whenever the thought of a drink arises. Many of us do, but others have sound health reasons for avoiding sweets. However, fresh fruit and dietetic substitutes for sweet food and drink are available, and so the idea of using a sweet *taste* is practical for anyone.

Some of us think it is more than the taste that helps quell the impulse toward alcohol. It may also be, in part, just substituting a new set of physical actions: getting a soft drink, a glass of milk or punch, and some cookies or some ice cream, then drinking or chewing, and swallowing.

Certainly, many alcoholics, when they first stop drinking, are found to be much more undernourished than they had suspected. (And the condition is encountered in all economic brackets.) For that reason, many of us are advised by our doctors to take supplemental vitamins. So perhaps many of us simply need nourishment more than we realize, and any good food in the stomach really makes us feel better physiologically. A hamburger, honey, peanuts, raw vegetables, cheese, nuts, cold shrimp, fruit gelatin, a mint—anything you like, that is good for you, can do the trick.

Newly sober alcoholics, when it is suggested they eat instead of drink, frequently wonder: What about getting too fat? We can point out that we see this occur only rarely. Many of us lose unnecessary fat when we start taking in wholesome food instead of the sheer calories of ethyl alcohol, and others have gained needed pounds.

To be sure, a few ice cream or candy "addicts" do find in their first sober months a bulge or roll developing here and there, in the usual wrong places. But that seems a small price to pay for release from active alcoholism. Better to be chubby or pleasingly plump than drunk, right? Did you ever hear of anyone being arrested for "fat driving"?

Anyhow, with a little patience and sound judgment, the weight situation usually straightens itself out, our experience proves. If it does not, or if you have a chronic, serious obesity or underweight problem, you probably should consult a medical expert who not only knows weight problems, but also understands alcoholism. We never find any conflict between A.A. experience and sound medical advice given by a physician sophisticated about alcoholism.

So the next time the temptation to drink arises, let's eat a little, or sip something gooey. At least, that puts off the drink for an hour or two, so we can take another step toward recovery... maybe the one suggested in the next section.

10 Making use of 'telephone therapy'

When we were first trying to achieve sobriety, many of us found ourselves taking a drink without planning to. Sometimes, it seemed to happen practically without our knowing it. There was no conscious decision to drink, and there was no real thought about possible consequences. We had not intended to set off an entire drinking episode.

Now we have learned that simply postponing that first drink, putting something else in its place, provides us with a chance to *think* about our drinking history, to think about the disease of alcoholism, and to think about the probable results of starting to drink.

Fortunately, we can do more than just think about it, and we do. We telephone someone.

When we stopped drinking, we were told repeatedly to get A.A. people's telephone numbers, and instead of drinking, to phone these people.

At first, the thought of telephoning a new acquaintance, someone we barely knew, seemed strange, and most of us were reluctant. But the A.A.'s—those with more nondrinking days behind them than we had—kept suggesting it. They said they understood why we hesitated, because they had felt the same way. Nevertheless, they said, just *try* it, at least once.

And so, finally, thousands and thousands of us have. To our relief, it turned out to be an easy, pleasant experience. Best of all, it worked.

Maybe the quickest way to understand this, before you try it, is to put yourself mentally in the place of the person being called. It is a rewarding and gratifying thing to be trusted that much. So the person receiving the call is almost invariably nice, even charming, about it— not at all surprised, and even glad to hear from us.

There's more. Lots of us have found that when we wanted to drink, we could telephone someone more experienced in sobriety than we were, and it was not even necessary to mention that we were thinking of drinking. That was often understood, without a word. *And it really did not matter what time we called, day or nights!*

Sometimes, for no apparent reason, we found ourselves suddenly, inexplicably undergoing an onslaught of anxiety, fear, terror, even panic, which made no sense. (This happens to lots of human beings, of course, not just to alcoholics.)

When we told the truth about the way we really felt, what we were doing, and what we wanted to do, we found we were perfectly understood. We got total empathy—not sympathy. Everyone we called, remember, had been in exactly the same boat some time or other, and they all remembered, vividly.

More frequently than not, only a few moments of conversation made our thought of a drink disappear. Sometimes, we got practical, eye-opening information, or gentle, indirect guidance, or tough, direct, heart-to-heart advice. Sometimes, we found ourselves laughing.

Observers of recovered alcoholics have noticed the extensive network of informal social contacts among A.A. members, even when we are not at A.A. meetings, and often when no one is thinking or talking of drinking. We've found we can have about as much social life with each other as we want, doing together the usual things friends do—listening to music, gabbing, going to plays and movies, eating together, camping and fishing, sight-seeing, or just visiting, in person or by note or telephone-all without the necessity of a single drink.

Such acquaintanceships and friendships have a unique value for those of us who choose not to drink. We are free to be ourselves among people who share our own concern for the maintenance of a happy sobriety, without being fanatically against all drinking.

It is possible, of course, to remain sober among people who are not recovered alcoholics, and even among those who drink a lot, though we will probably feel some social discomfort in their company. But among other sober alcoholics, we can be sure that our recovery from alcoholism is highly prized and deeply understood. It means a lot to these friends, just as their health is cherished by us.

The transition to enjoyment of sobriety sometimes begins when, newly sober, we keep in touch with others equally new at the game. At first, it often seems a little awkward to strike up friendships with people who have been sober for years. We are usually more at ease with those who, like ourselves, are just setting out toward recovery. That's why many of us make our first telephone calls about not drinking to our A.A. "contemporaries."

"Telephone therapy" works even when we don't know any individual to call. Since a number for A.A. is listed in practically every telephone directory in the United States and Canada (and in many other countries), it is easy simply to dial that number and instantly be in touch with someone who honestly understands, at gut level. It may be a person we have never met, but the same genuine empathy is there.

Once the first call is made, it is much, much easier to make another, when it is needed. Finally, the need to talk away a desire for a drink virtually disappears for most of us. When it does, though, many of us find we have established a habit of occasional friendly telephone visits, so we keep them up because we enjoy them.

But that usually comes later. At first, "telephone therapy" is primarily for helping us stay sober. We reach for the phone instead of a drink. Even when we don't think it will work. Even when we don't want to.

11 Availing yourself of a sponsor

Not every A.A. member has had a sponsor. But thousands of us say we would not be alive were it not for the special friendship of one recovered alcoholic in the first months and years of our sobriety.

In the earliest days of A.A., the term "sponsor" was not in the A.A. jargon. Then a few hospitals in Akron, Ohio, and New York began to accept alcoholics (under that diagnosis) as patients—*if* a sober A.A. member would agree to "sponsor" the sick man or woman. The sponsor took the patient to the hospital, visited him or her regularly, was present when the patient was discharged, and took the patient home and then to an A.A. meeting. At the meeting, the sponsor introduced the newcomer to other happily nondrinking alcoholics. All through the early months of recovery, the sponsor stood by, ready to answer questions or to listen whenever needed.

Sponsorship turned out to be such a good way to help people get established in A.A. that it has become a custom followed throughout the A.A. world, even when hospitalization is not necessary.

Often, the sponsor is the first person to call on a problem drinker who wants help—or the first recovered alcoholic to talk with the inquirer if he or she goes to an A.A. office—or the A.A. member volunteering to "sponsor" an alcoholic about to be released from a detox or rehab unit, a hospital, or a correctional facility.

At A.A. meetings, people often recommend that an A.A. beginner get a sponsor, and it is left up to the newcomer to pick someone as his or her sponsor, if one is wanted.

One reason it is a good idea to have a sponsor is that you have a friendly guide during those first days and weeks when A.A. seems strange and new, before you feel you know your own way about. Besides, a sponsor can spend far more time with you, and give you far more individual attention, than a busy professional helper possibly could. Sponsors make house calls, even at night.

If you do have a sponsor, some of the following suggestions may help. Remember, they are based on thousands of A.A. members' experience over many, many years.

A. It's usually better if men sponsor men and women sponsor women. This helps avoid the possibility of romance rearing its lovely head—a development which can hideously complicate, if not destroy, the sponsor-newcomer relationship. By trial and error, we've discovered that sex and sponsorship are a very bad mix.

B. Whether or not we like what our sponsor suggests (and sponsors can only suggest; they cannot make anybody do anything, or actually prevent any action), the fact is that the sponsor has been sober longer, knows pitfalls to avoid, and may be right.

C. An A.A. sponsor is not a professional caseworker or counselor of any sort. A sponsor is not someone to borrow money from, nor get clothes, jobs, or food from. A sponsor is not a medical expert, nor qualified to give religious, legal, domestic, or psychiatric advice, although a good sponsor is usually willing to discuss such matters confidentially, and often can suggest where the appropriate professional assistance can be obtained.

A sponsor is simply a sober alcoholic who can help solve only one problem: how to stay sober. And the sponsor has only one tool to use—personal experience, not scientific wisdom.

Sponsors have *been* there, and they often have more concern, hope, compassion, and confidence for us than we have for ourselves. They certainly have had more experience. Remembering their own condition, they reach *out* to help, not down.

Someone has said alcoholics may be people who should never keep secrets about themselves, especially the guilty kind. Being open about ourselves helps prevent that, and can be a good antidote for any tendency toward excessive self-concern and self-consciousness. A good sponsor is someone we can confide in, get everything off our chests with.

D. It's agreeable when the sponsor is congenial, someone who shares our background and interests beyond sobriety. But it is not necessary. In many instances, the best sponsor is someone totally different. The most unlikely pairings of sponsor and newcomer sometimes work the best.

E. Sponsors, like most everyone else, are likely to have some family and job obligations. Although a sponsor will, on occasion, leave work or home to help a newcomer in a real bind, there are naturally times when the sponsor is truly out of reach.

Here is the opportunity for many of us to use our reawakening wits and figure out a substitute for a sponsor. If we genuinely desire help, we do not let a sponsor's illness, or momentary unavailability for any other reason, stop us from getting some help.

We can try to find a nearby A.A. meeting. We can read A.A. literature or something else we have found helpful. We can telephone other recovered alcoholics we have met, even if we don't know them very well. And we can telephone or visit the nearest A.A. office or clubroom for A.A. members.

Even if the only person we find to talk to is someone we have not met before, we're sure to encounter sincere interest and a desire to help in any A.A. member we reach. When we really level about our distress, true empathy is forthcoming. Sometimes, we get really needed encouragement from recovered alcoholics we do not much care for. Even if such a feeling is mutual, when one of us trying to stay sober asks any other recovered alcoholic to help us not drink, all petty and superficial differences melt away.

F. Some people think it a good idea to have more than one sponsor, so at least one is always likely to be available. This plan has one additional advantage, but also carries a slight risk.

The advantage is that three or four sponsors provide a wider range of experience and knowledge than any one person possibly can.

The risk in having several sponsors, rather than just one, lies in a tendency some of us developed during our drinking days. In order to protect ourselves and keep our drinking beyond criticism, we often told different tales to different people. We even learned how to manipulate people, in a sense, so the people-environment would practically condone, or even encourage, our drinking. We may not have been aware of this tendency, and it was usually lacking in any evil intent. But it really became a part of our personalities in our drinking days.

So a few of us with a clutch of sponsors have caught ourselves trying to play off one sponsor against another, telling one thing to the first, something else to the second. This doesn't always work, since sponsors are hard to kid. They catch on pretty fast to the tricks of anyone wanting to drink, having used almost all such wiles themselves. But sometimes we can keep at it until we get one sponsor to say something directly opposite to what another sponsor has said. Maybe we manage to wangle out of somebody what we *want* to hear, not what we need. Or, at least, we interpret this sponsor's words to suit our wishes.

Such behavior seems more a reflection of our illness than an honest search for help in getting well. We, the newcomers, are the ones most hurt when this happens. So maybe if we have a team of sponsors, it would be a good idea to keep one eye cocked sharply, alert to catch ourselves if we should find ourselves getting into games like that, instead of trying to progress straight toward our own recovery goal.

G. Being recovered alcoholics themselves, sponsors naturally have their own unique strengths—and foibles. The sponsor (or any other human being) without flaw or weakness hasn't turned up yet, as far as we know.

It is a rare occurrence, but it is possible that we can be misled or given a bum steer by a sponsor's mistaken advice. As we've all found by doing it ourselves, even with the best intentions, sponsors can goof.

You probably can guess what the next sentence will say.... *A sponsor's unfortunate behavior is no more a valid excuse for taking a drink than anything else is.* The hand that pours a drink down your gullet is still your own.

Rather than blame the sponsor, we've found at least 30 other ways to stay away from a drink. Those 30 are laid out in the other sections of this booklet, of course.

H. You are under no obligation ever to repay your sponsor in any way for helping you. He or she does so because helping others helps us maintain our own sobriety. You are free to accept or reject help. If you accept it, you have no debt to repay.

Sponsors are kind—and tough—not for credit, and not because they like to "do good works." A good sponsor is as much helped as the person being sponsored. You'll find this to be true the first time you sponsor someone.

Some day, you may want to pass such help on to someone else. That's the only thanks you need give.

I. Like a good parent, a wise sponsor can let the newcomer alone, when necessary; can let the newcomer make his or her own mistakes; can see the newcomer rejecting advice and still not get angry or feel spurned. A sharp sponsor tries hard to keep vanity and hurt feelings out of the way in sponsorship.

And the best sponsors are really delighted when the newcomer is able to step out past the stage of being sponsored. Not that we ever have to go it altogether alone. But the time does come when even a young bird must use its own wings and start its own family. Happy flying!

12 Getting plenty of rest

For at least three reasons, people who drink heavily often cannot realize how tired they are. The reasons are three characteristics of alcohol: (1) It is full of calories, which give instant energy; (2) it numbs the central nervous system, so that one cannot fully feel body discomfort; (3) after its anesthetic effect wears off, it produces agitation that *feels* like nervous energy.

After we stop drinking, the agitating effect may persist for a while, leading to jumpiness and insomnia. Or we may suddenly become aware of our fatigue and so feel worn-out and lethargic. Or the two conditions may alternate.

Either is a normal reaction that thousands of us have had at the very beginning of our sobriety, in degrees depending on our previous drinking and general state of health. Both wear off sooner or later and need not cause any alarm.

But it is very important to get plenty of rest when we stop drinking, because the notion of having a drink seems to arrive from nowhere with greater ease when we are tired.

Many of us have wondered why we suddenly feel like taking a drink, for no apparent reason. When we examine the situation, time after time we find that we are feeling exhausted and hadn't realized it. Chances are, we have used up too much energy and have not had enough rest. Generally, a snack of some kind or a little nap can change our feelings completely, and the idea of a drink vanishes. Even if we can't fall asleep, just a few minutes of lying down, or relaxing in a chair or a tub, take the edge off the fatigue.

It's even better, of course, to get our lives on a healthy schedule which permits a sufficient regular rest period every 24 hours.

Not all, but thousands of us can tell stories of insomnia spells after we quit drinking. Evidently, it takes a little while for the nervous system to learn (or usually to relearn) the habit of regular, undisturbed sleep without alcohol in the body. What may be the worst part of this is our worry about it, because the worrying makes it even harder to get to sleep.

The first advice we commonly give each other on this point is "Don't worry. Nobody has ever died of lack of sleep. When your body is tired enough, you'll sleep." And so it turns out.

Since insomnia was so often the excuse many of us gave ourselves for "needing a drink or two," we largely agree that a brand-new attitude toward insomnia helps in trying not to drink. Rather than toss and turn and fret about it, some of us give in to it, get up, and get some reading and writing done in the wee hours.

Meanwhile, it is a good idea to check out our other health habits to see whether we are in any way making sleep difficult for ourselves. Too much caffeine in the evenings? Are we eating properly? Getting enough of the right kind of exercise? Is the digestive system functioning properly yet? That may take some time.

Many simple, old-fashioned recipes for insomnia actually help, such as a glass of hot milk, deep breathing, a soak in a warm tub, a dull book, or some soft music. Some prefer more exotic gimmicks. One recovered alcoholic recommends heated ginger ale with pepper in it! (To each his or her own!) Others rely on a particular massage, yoga, or various remedies suggested in books on the subject.

Even if we do not fall asleep at once, we can rest by lying still with the eyes closed. Nobody goes to sleep pacing a room or talking all night over coffee.

If the condition persists, it may be advisable to check with a good physician who understands alcoholism well.

One thing we have learned for sure: *Sleeping medicines of any sort are not the answer for alcoholics.* They almost invariably lead to drinking, our experience repeatedly shows.

Because we know how dangerous such medicines can be, some of us have had to put up with slight discomfort for a little while, until our bodies settled into a healthy sleep routine. Once we are past the temporary unease, when a natural sleep rhythm sets in, we can see that the price was eminently worth it.

One more curious item about sleep after we stop drinking may be useful. Long after we have weaned ourselves from the bottle, a great many of us are startled to awaken some morning or night realizing we have just had an all-too-vivid dream about drinking.

Not all of us have such dreams. But enough have for us to know that they are common, and harmless.

A.A. is not a program of dream interpretation, so we cannot point out the hidden meanings, if any, that such dreams have, as psychoanalysts and other dream interpreters do. We can report only that such dreams may occur, so don't be too surprised. Among the most common is a dream that one finds oneself drunk, and horrified about it, but has no memory at all of taking a drink. We may even awaken with chills, shakes, and other classic hangover jitters—when, of course, we haven't touched a drop in months. It was all just a bad dream. And it may come out of the blue, long, long after our last drink.

Probably, it's a good thing that we find ourselves shook up and miserable at the notion of drinking, even in a dream. Maybe this means we are really beginning to get the idea, deep down in our bones, that drinking is no good for us. Sobriety is better, even to dream about.

The beauty of sober sleep, once it is achieved, is the sheer pleasure of waking up—no real hangover, no worries about what may have happened in last night's blackout. Instead, it means facing the new day refreshed, hopeful, and grateful.

13 'First Things First'

Here's an old saying that has special, strong meaning for us. Simply stated, it is this: Above all other concerns, we must remember that we cannot drink. Not drinking is the first order of business for us, anywhere, any time, under any circumstances.

This is strictly a matter of survival for us. We have learned that alcoholism is a killer disease, leading to death in a large number of ways. We prefer not to activate that disease by risking a drink.

Treatment of our condition, as the American Medical Association has noted, "primarily involves not taking a drink." Our experience reinforces that prescription for therapy.

In practical, day-by-day matters, this means we must take whatever steps are necessary, at whatever inconvenience, *not* to drink.

Some have asked us, "Does this mean you rank sobriety ahead of family, job, and the opinion of friends?"

When we view alcoholism as the life-or-death matter it is, the answer is plain. If we do not save our health—our lives—then certainly we will have no family, no job, and no friends. If we value family, job, and friends, we must *first* save our own lives in order to cherish all three.

"First Things First" is rich in other meanings, too, which can be significant in combating our drinking problem. For instance, many of us have noticed that when we first stopped drinking, it seemed to take us longer to make up our minds than we liked. Decisions seemed to come hard—on again, then off again.

Now, indecisiveness is certainly not limited to recovering alcoholics, but perhaps it bothered us more than it would others. The newly sober homemaker could not figure out which of many cleanup jobs to do first. The businessman couldn't decide whether to return those phone calls or dictate those letters. In many departments of our lives, we wanted to catch up on all the tasks and obligations we had been neglecting. Obviously, we couldn't take care of them all at once.

So "First Things First" helped. If any of the choices before us involved drinking or not drinking, that decision deserved and got priority. Unless we held on to our sobriety, we knew, *no* cleaning would get done, no calls made, no letters written.

Then we used the same slogan in ordering our newfound sober time. We tried planning the day's activities, arranging our tasks in order of importance, and never making the schedule too tight. We kept in mind another "first," our general health, because we knew that getting overtired or skipping meals could be dangerous.

During active alcoholism, many of us led pretty disorganized lives, and the confusion often made us feel unsettled or even desperate. Learning not to drink is facilitated, we have discovered, by introducing some order into each day—but being realistic and keeping our plan flexible. The rhythm of our own special routine has a soothing effect, and an apt principle around which to organize some orderliness is—yes, "First Things First."

14 Fending off loneliness

Alcoholism has been described as "the lonely disease," and very few recovered alcoholics argue the point. Looking back at the last years or months of our drinking, literally hundreds of thousands* of us remember feeling isolated even when we were among a lot of happy, celebrating people. We often felt a deep sense of not belonging, even when we cheerfully acted sociable.

Many of us have said we drank originally to be "a part of the crowd." Many of us felt we had to drink to "get in," and to feel that we fitted in with the rest of the human race.

It is an observable fact, of course, that our chief use of alcohol was egocentric—that is, we poured it into our *own* bodies, for the effect we felt within our *own* skin. Sometimes, that effect momentarily helped us to behave sociably, or temporarily assuaged our inner lonesomeness.

---

* The present worldwide membership of A.A. is estimated to be over two million.

But when that effect of alcohol wore off, we were left feeling more set apart, more left out, more "different" than ever, and sadder.

If we felt guilty or ashamed of either our drunkenness itself or anything we did while drinking, that compounded our feeling of being an outcast. At times, we secretly feared or even believed that we deserved ostracism, because of the things we did. "Maybe," many of us thought, "I really am an outsider."

(Perhaps this feeling is familiar to you, when you think back to your last bad hangover or bad drunk.)

The lonely road ahead looked bleak, dark, and unending. It was too painful to talk about; and to avoid thinking about it, we soon drank again.

Although some of us were lone drinkers, it can hardly be said that we completely lacked companionship during our drinking days. People were all around us. We saw, heard, and touched them. But most of our important dialogues were entirely interior, held with ourselves. We were sure nobody else would understand. Besides, considering our opinion of ourselves, we were not sure that we *wanted* anybody to understand.

No wonder, then, that when we first listen to recovered alcoholics in A.A. talking freely and honestly about themselves, we are stunned. Their tales of their own drinking escapades, of their own secret fears and loneliness, jar us like a thunderbolt.

We discover—but can hardly dare to believe right at first—that *we are not alone.* We are *not* totally unlike *everybody,* after all.

The brittle shell of protective and fearful egocentricity we have dwelled in so long is cracked open by the honesty of other recovered alcoholics. We sense, almost before we can articulate it, that we do belong somewhere, and the loneliness starts rapidly leaking away.

Relief is too weak a word to convey our initial feeling. It is mixed with wonder, too, and almost a kind of terror. Is it real? Will this last?

Those of us sober in A.A. a few years can assure any newcomer at an A.A. meeting that it *is* real, very real indeed. And it does last. It is not just another false start, of the sort that most of us have experienced too often. It is not one more burst of gladness soon to be followed by hurt disappointment.

Instead, as the number of people now sober for decades in A.A. swells each year, we see before our eyes more and more hard proof that we can have a genuine and enduring recovery from the loneliness of alcoholism.

Still, getting over years-long, deeply ingrained habits of suspicion and other protective mechanisms can hardly be an overnight process. We have become thoroughly conditioned to feeling and acting misunderstood and unloved—whether we really were or not. We are accustomed to acting like loners. So, after we first stop drinking, some of us may need a little time and a little practice to break out of our customary solitude. Even though we begin to believe we are not alone any more, we sometimes act and feel in the old ways.

We're green at reaching out for friendship—or even accepting it when it is offered. We're not quite sure how to do it, or whether it will work. And that piled-up, superheavy burden of years of fear still can drag at us. Therefore, when we start to feel a bit lonely—whether we are actually, physically alone or not—the old routines and the balm of booze can easily entice us.

Now and then, some of us are even tempted just to give up, and go back to the old misery. At least, it is familiar, and we wouldn't have to work hard to recapture all the expertise we achieved at the drinking life.

Telling an A.A. group about himself, a fellow once said that being a drunk from his teen-age years to his forties was a full-time occupation, and he passed by most of the things North American males usually learn as they grow into young manhood.

So there he was in his forties, he said, sober. He knew how to drink and brawl, but he had never learned a vocational or professional skill, and he was ignorant of most social graces. "It was awful," he declared. "I didn't even know how to ask a girl for a date or what to do on one! And I found there aren't any classes on 'How to Date' for 40-year-old bachelors who never learned."

The laughter in the A.A. meeting room that night was particularly hearty and affectionate. So many there empathized, had gone through the same brand of unease. When we feel such awkwardness, incongruous at 40 (or even at 20, these days), we might think we were pathetic, even grotesque—were it not for the many rooms full of understanding A.A. people who have known that very type of fear, and can now help us see the humor in it. So we can smile as we try again, until we get it right. We do not have to give up in secret shame any more; we do not have to renew our old, hopeless attempts to find social confidence in the bottle, where we found loneliness instead.

That is just one extreme example of the kind of all-arms-and-legs feeling some of us get when we first set sail on sobriety. It illustrates how dangerously lost we might be if we tried to go it alone. There might be one chance in millions that we'd make the voyage somehow.

But we know now that we do not have to proceed all on our own. It is far more sensible, safer, and surer to do it in the company of the whole happy fleet going in the same direction. And none of us need feel any shame at all at using help, since we all help each other.

It is no more cowardly to use help in recovering from a drinking problem than it is to use a crutch if you have a broken leg. A crutch is a beautiful thing to those who need it, and to those who see its usefulness.

Is there really anything heroic in a sightless person's stumbling and groping—just because he or she refuses to use easily obtained assistance? Foolish risk-taking—even when it is not at all necessary—sometimes does get undeserved praise. But mutual helpfulness—since it always works better—really should be more prized and admired.

Our own experience at staying sober overwhelmingly reflects the wisdom of using whatever good help is available in recovery from a drinking problem. Despite our great need and desire, none of us recovered from alcoholism solely on our own. If we had, of course, we would have had no need to approach A.A., a psychiatrist, or anyone else for aid.

Since no one can live totally alone, since all of us are dependent to some degree on our fellow human beings for at least some goods and services, we have found it sensible to accept that particular reality, and to work within it in the highly important venture of getting over our active alcoholism.

Thoughts of a drink seem to sneak into our minds much more smoothly and slyly when we are alone. And when we feel lonesome, and an urge for a drink strikes, it seems to have special speed and strength.

Such ideas and desires are much less likely to occur when we are with other people, especially other nondrinkers. If they do occur, they seem less potent and more easily put aside while we are in touch with fellow A.A. members.

We are not forgetting that almost everyone occasionally needs some time to himself, or herself, to collect thoughts, take stock, get some thing done, work out a private situation, or just vacation from the stress of the usual day. But we have found it dangerous to become too indulgent about this, especially when our mood becomes a bit morose or self-pitying. Almost any company is better than a bitter privacy.

Of course, even at an A.A. meeting, it is possible to want to drink, just as people can feel lonely in a crowd. But the odds against taking the drink are much better in the company of other A.A.'s than they are when we are alone in our room, or in a hidden corner of a quiet, deserted barroom.

When we have only ourselves to talk to, the conversation gets kind of circular. More and more, it excludes the sort of sensible input other people can supply. Trying to argue yourself out of a drink is rather like attempting self-hypnosis. Often, it is about as effective as trying to persuade a pregnant mare not to foal when her term has come.

For these reasons, then, when we suggest avoiding fatigue and hunger, we often tie in a mention of one more hazard to make it a triple play: "Don't let yourself get too tired, too hungry, or too lonely."

Check it out.

If the notion of taking a drink crosses your mind any time soon, pause to consider. As often as not, you are likely to find you are in one or more of those three high-risk conditions.

Tell somebody, fast. That at least starts to relieve the loneliness.

15 Watching out for anger and resentments

Anger has already been touched on in this booklet, but some rough experiences have convinced us it is so important it deserves special attention from anyone wanting to get over a drinking problem.

Hostility, resentment, anger—whatever word you use to describe this feeling—seems to have a close tie-up with intoxication and maybe even a deeper one with alcoholism.

For instance, some scientists once asked a large number of alcoholic men why they got drunk, and found an important answer was "So I can tell somebody off." In other words, they felt the power and freedom while drunk to express anger they could not comfortably display when sober.

Someone has suggested there may be a subtle, undetermined biochemical relationship between alcohol and the kind of body changes that accompany anger. One experimental study of alcoholics suggested that resentments may create in the blood of alcoholics a certain uncomfortable condition that is cleared up by a binge. A top psychologist has recently suggested that drinkers may enjoy the feelings of power over others that the influence of alcohol can bring.

Facts have been reported about the close correlation between drinking and assaults and homicides. It seems a large proportion of these in some countries happen when either the victim or the perpetrator (or both) is under the influence of alcohol. Rapes, domestic squabbles leading to divorce, child abuse, and armed robbery are also frequently laid at the doorstep of excessive drinking.

Even those of us who have had no experience in such behavior can easily understand the kind of fierce rage which might lead some people to think of such violence when they are tight enough. So we recognize the potential danger in anger.

There seems little doubt that it is a natural state to occur in the human animal from time to time. Like fear, it may well have some survival value for all members of species *homo sapiens.* Anger toward abstractions such as poverty, hunger, illness, and injustice have no doubt produced changes for the better in various cultures.

But there is also no denying that mayhem and even verbal assaults committed in excesses of anger are deplorable and do damage to society as a whole, as well as to individuals. Therefore, many religions and philosophies urge us to get rid of anger in order to find a happier life.

Yet a great number of people are certain that bottling up anger is very bad for emotional health, that we should get our hostility out in some way, or it will "poison" our insides by turning inward toward ourselves, thus leading to deep depression.

Anger in all its aspects is a universal human problem. But it poses a special threat to alcoholics: Our own anger can kill us. Recovered alcoholics almost unanimously agree that hostility, grudges, or resentments often make us want to drink, so we need to be vigilant against such feelings. We have found much more satisfying ways than drinking for dealing with them.

But we'll get to those later. First, here is a look at some of the shapes and colors anger seems at times to arrive in:

intolerance	snobbishness	tension	distrust
contempt	rigidity	sarcasm	anxiety
envy	cynicism	self-pity	suspicion
hatred	discontent	malice	jealousy

Various A.A. members have, when sober, been able to trace all those feelings to some underlying anger. During our drinking days, many of us spent little time thinking such things out. We were more likely to brood about them, or to overreact, especially after we heightened such feelings by taking another drink.

Perhaps fear should be on that list, too, because many of us believe anger is frequently an outgrowth of fear. We're not always sure *what* we're afraid of; sometimes, it is just a vague, generalized, nameless fear. And it can give rise to an equally generalized anger, which may suddenly focus on something or someone.

Feelings of frustration also can give birth to anger. As a class, problem drinkers are not famous for a high tolerance level when faced with frustration, real or imaginary. A drink used to be our favorite solvent for such an indigestible emotion.

Perhaps "justifiable" resentment is the trickiest of all to handle. It's the end product of "righteous" anger, after long cherishing, and if it is allowed to continue, it will slowly undermine our defenses against taking a drink.

Even if we actually have been treated shabbily or unjustly, resentment is a luxury that, as alcoholics, we cannot afford. For us, *all* anger is self-destructive, because it can lead us back to drinking.

(Learning to deal with resentments is discussed in more detail in the books "Alcoholics Anonymous" and "Twelve Steps and Twelve Traditions.")

We cannot pretend to be experts at understanding depth psychology, so we have to concentrate at first, not on searching for the causes of uncomfortable feelings of anger, but on coping with the feelings themselves, whether or not we think they are justified. We zero in on how to keep such feelings from fooling us into taking a drink.

Interestingly, several of the methods already discussed for avoiding a drink have also worked splendidly for getting over the inner discomfort we suffer when angry. For instance, when we begin to simmer inside, it sometimes helps a great deal to take a few bites of something good to eat, or a glass of a sweetened, nonintoxicating beverage.

It's also remarkably effective, when we begin to get teed off at something, to pick up the phone and talk about it to our sponsor or to other recovered alcoholics. And it pays to pause and consider whether or not we may be overtired. If so, we've found that some rest often dissipates rage.

Repeatedly, simply pondering "Live and Let Live" cools our temper.

Or we may shift quickly to an activity that has nothing to do with the source of our anger—work it off with some lively exercise—lose it in listening to our favorite music.

For many of us, contemplating the ideas of the Serenity Prayer blows away our hostility. Often, whatever we are mad about turns out to be something we cannot possibly control or change (traffic jams, the weather, long supermarket lines, for example), so the sensible, mature thing to do is just accept it, rather than boil inside fruitlessly or turn to alcohol.

Of course, at times we are resentful of a circumstance in our life that can, and should, be changed. Maybe we *should* quit a job and get a better one, or get a divorce, or move the family to a different neighborhood. If so, such a decision needs to be made carefully, not in haste or anger. So we still should cool down first. Then maybe we can give some calm, constructive thought to figuring out whether our resentment is directed at something we can change. To double-check this, see the section on the Serenity Prayer, page 18.

Sometimes, it isn't long resentment we must deal with, but a sudden, consuming rage. The 24-hour plan (page 5) and "First Things First" (page 32) have helped many of us cope with such a rage, although we didn't see how they possibly could until we actually tried them—and got surprisingly good results.

Another effective remedy for anger is the "as if" idea. We decide how a mature, truly well-balanced person would ideally handle a resentment like ours, then act *as if* we were that person. Have a go at it a few times. It works, too.

And for many of us, so does the professional guidance of a good counselor of some sort, a psychiatrist or other physician, or a clergyman.

We can also find an outlet in harmless physical action. The exercise already mentioned, deep breathing, a hot soak, and (in private) pounding a chair or a cushion and yelling have all relieved anger for lots of people.

Simply repressing, glossing over, or damming up anger rarely seems advisable. Instead, we try to learn not to act *on* it, but to do something *about* it. If we don't, we increase enormously our chances of drinking.

As laymen who know simply our own experience, we recovered alcoholics have no laboratory knowledge or scientific theories about these matters. But few people who have ever had a hangover could forget how unreasonably irritable it makes you feel. Sometimes, we took it out on family members, fellow workers, friends, or strangers who certainly had not earned our displeasure. That tendency can hang around awhile after we start staying sober, the way wraiths of stale smoke do in a closed-up barroom, reminding us of drinking days—until we do a good mental housecleaning.

16 Being good to yourself

When a loved one or a dear friend of ours is recuperating from a serious illness, we generally try to give what good nurses call T.L.C. (Tender Loving Care). We pamper a sick child, providing favorite foods and some fun to help in recovery.

Convalescence from the illness of active alcoholism takes some time, and anyone going through it deserves consideration and a measure of T.L.C.

In times past, people often believed that those recovering from certain ailments just deserved to suffer, since it was thought they had deliberately, selfishly inflicted the sickness on themselves.

Because of the guilt and stigma still laid on alcoholism by people who are ignorant of the nature of the disease (including ourselves before we learned better), many of us were not very kind to ourselves in the throes of a hangover. We just suffered and thought of ourselves as "paying the piper" in necessary penance for our misdeeds.

Now that we know alcoholism is not immoral behavior, we have found it essential to readjust our attitudes. We have learned that one of the persons *least* likely to treat the alcoholic like a sick person is, somewhat surprisingly, the alcoholic herself (or himself). Once again, our old thinking habits are cropping up.

It's often said that problem drinkers are perfectionists, impatient about any shortcomings, especially our own. Setting impossible goals for ourselves, we nevertheless struggle fiercely to reach these unattainable ideals.

Then, since no human being could possibly maintain the extremely high standards we often demand, we find ourselves falling short, as all people must whose aims are unrealistic. And discouragement and depression set in. We angrily punish ourselves for being less than super-perfect.

That is precisely where we can start being good—at least fair—to ourselves. We would not demand of a child or of any handicapped person more than is reasonable. It seems to us we have no right to expect such miracles of ourselves as recovering alcoholics, either.

Impatient to get completely well by Tuesday, we find ourselves still convalescing on Wednesday, and start blaming ourselves. That's a good time to back off, mentally, and look at ourselves in as detached, objective a way as we can. What would we do if a sick loved one or friend got discouraged about slow recuperation progress, and began to refuse medicine?

It helps to remember that heavy drinking is highly damaging to the body, producing conditions which can take months or years to get over. No one becomes an alcoholic in just a few weeks (well, *almost* no one). We cannot expect to recover in a magic instant, either.

When feelings of discouragement come, we then need to encourage ourselves. More than one of us have found it good medicine to give ourselves a pat on the back, to salute the progress already made—without being smug or dangerously egotistical about it, of course.

Take stock. Have we refrained from taking a drink this 24 hours? That deserves honest self-commendation. Have we made ourselves eat properly today? Have we tried to fulfill our obligations today? Have we, in short, done about the best we could, and all we could, today? If so, that's all it is fair to expect.

Maybe we can't answer yes to all those questions. Maybe we have fallen short somehow, backslid a bit in our thinking or actions, despite knowing better. So what? We are not perfect creatures. We should settle for small progress, rather than bemoan any lack of perfection.

What can we do right now to cheer ourselves up? We can do something *other* than take a drink. Every section of this booklet makes suggestions of that sort.

But there is more, perhaps. Have we been enjoying life lately? Or have we been so concerned about getting better, kept our nose so earnestly near the grindstone of self-improvement, that we have failed to enjoy a sunset? A new moon? A good meal? A needed holiday from care? A good joke? Some affection?

Since the body seeks to normalize itself, maybe yours will welcome opportunities for needed rest. Enjoy deliciously drowsy naps, or good, long nights of peaceful slumber. Or perhaps you have left-over energy you can use in pure fun and enjoyment. As much as other aspects of life, these seem necessary for fulfilling our entire human potential.

Now is the time, the only time there is. And if we are not kind to ourselves right now, we certainly cannot rightfully expect respect or consideration from others.

We have found we can enjoy, sober, every good thing we enjoyed while drinking—and many, many more. It takes a little practice, but the rewards more than make up for the effort. To do so is not selfish, but self-protective. Unless we cherish our own recovery, we cannot survive to become unselfish, ethical, and socially responsible people.

17 Looking out for overelation

A great many drinkers (whether alcoholics or not) change an internal state of discomfort to one of enjoyment by the single act of taking a drink. This method of fleeing from pain to pleasure has been described as "escape drinking."

But thousands and thousands of us know that often we were already in a happy frame of mind when we took a drink. In fact, when we review our drinking records carefully, large numbers of us can see that we often drank in order to intensify an already jubilant mood.

This experience gives rise to our next suggestion, which is: Be especially cautious during moments of celebration or times of just feeling extraordinarily good.

When things are going great, so well you feel almost on a nonalcoholic high—look out! At such times (even after several years of sobriety), the thought of a drink may seem quite natural, and the misery of our old drinking days temporarily dims. Just one drink begins to seem less threatening, and we start thinking that it wouldn't be fatal, or even harmful.

Sure enough, *one* would not be—for the average person. But our experience with a drinking problem shows us what that one supposedly harmless, fateful drink would do to us *un*average people. Sooner or later, it would persuade us that one more could do no damage, either. Then how about a couple more?...

Ceremonial, celebratory drinking seems particularly tempting to some of us when we have valid cause for exhilaration among jovial drinking relatives or friends who can drink safely. Their imbibing seems to exert social pressure on us to try to do likewise.

Perhaps this is because taking a shot of ethanol (ethyl alcohol) has so long been closely associated in our culture with fun and good times (as well as some mournful events). The connections in our mind can persist even long after we have learned we do not *have* to drink any more.

We know now that there are many ways we can fend off this social pressure to drink, as described on page 67. Briefly, let us just be reminded that no situation gives us a "dispensation" from our alcoholism, the illness that is activated as soon as we start ingesting alcohol at any time, for any reason, or for no reason.

For some of us, the impulse to take a joyful drink when we are feeling particularly good is even more insidious when there is no particular event to celebrate, and no particular social pressure to drink. It can occur at the most unexpected times, and we may never understand the reasons for it.

We have learned now not to panic when the thought of a drink comes into the mind. After all, it is a natural thought for anyone to have in modern times, and especially understandable for those of us who have had extensive practice in the art.

But the *thought* of a drink is not necessarily the same thing as the *desire* for one, and neither need plunge us into gloom or fear. Both can be viewed simply as warning bells to remind us of the perils of alcoholism. The perils are forever, even when we feel so fine that we wonder whether it's really all right for anyone to feel as good as we do, now.

18 'Easy Does It'

Have you just this minute finished reading the previous section, and are you now rushing right into this one? Why? It may be that you need to put into practice the slogan "Easy Does It."

As alcoholics, we often tended to gulp drinks faster than other people did. And we were seldom likely to overlook the last few drops in the cocktail glass, or the last few slugs in the bottle.

Many of us have been amused at our seeming inability, even after many years of sobriety, to walk away from a half-finished cup of coffee or glass of soda. We sometimes find ourselves gulping the last swallow of a nonalcoholic drink, as if . . .

Perhaps most readers already get the point: It is not always easy for us to put down an unfinished page, chapter, or book we are reading. There seems to be almost a compulsion to go on to the end, instead of taking only a page or a chapter or two a day and leaving the rest for another session. Not that this tendency is altogether bad. In getting over a destructive obsession such as drinking, it's sensible to replace it with a benign one, such as a compulsion to seek more and more knowledge and help for a drinking problem.

So read on, if you like. It's a whole lot healthier than boozing.

But when you reach the end of this section, you might want to try something. Put this book aside and review your day. See how many times you could have slowed down a bit or taken things a little easier if you had thought of it.

The slogan "Easy Does It" is one way we A.A.'s remind each other that many of us have tendencies at times to overdo things, to rush heedlessly along, impatient with anything that slows us down. We find it hard to relax and savor life.

When one of us is in a dither to get something done or get somewhere in a hurry, a friend may gently remonstrate, "'Easy Does It,' remember?" Then there's often a flash of annoyance at the adviser. And that indicates the advice must have hit home, wouldn't you say?

Yes, we know that impatience today is by no means limited to alcoholics. As the rate of change in our civilization accelerates, more and more people feel pressed for time and harried to hurry up and catch up with... With what? With whom?

Such pressure does not push most drinkers into alcoholism, as anyone can see. Only a small percentage of drinkers develop our problem. But those of us who did often find we share a need to learn how to relax, how to pace ourselves in a healthy way, how to enjoy small gains and even the simple pleasures along the way—in short, how to enjoy the journey, instead of just fretting until we reach our destination. The horizon stays there. Sometimes, it pays to stand still and gaze at it, for the refreshment of the long look.

Some of us repeatedly find, too, that we have bitten off more than even a hippo could chew. We keep taking on more commitments than any one person could handle.

Probably, we could learn a great deal about this from certain recovered cardiac patients. Many of them manage to be vigorously and productively active in a measured way which avoids harassment, overexertion, and frantic enslavement to the clock.

Some of us work out routines to help us keep our goals realistically within the realm of possibility. We may make up a list of things we'd like to get done today, then deliberately discard half or more of it. Another day, another list.

Or we intentionally schedule things pretty far in advance, teaching ourselves to neglect them, just as deliberately, until their time comes.

Others of us find that lists and schedules can become tyrants, driving us to finish every item, no matter how much time and effort it takes. So we swear off lists for a while. No longer pushed by their dictatorship, we can learn to move at a more spontaneous, leisurely pace.

For a great many of us, sitting quietly alone for 15 or 20 minutes before starting each day's activities helps us set out in a relaxed, orderly frame of mind. Some of us use specific methods of prayer or meditation which we have found particularly well suited to this purpose. And maybe several times during a hectic day, we manage to sit undisturbed, with eyes closed, for a five-minute break, then resume work refreshed.

For some of us, it is easier to slow ourselves down if we have the help of another person. We may be unable to generate our own peace, but sometimes we can make ourselves sit quietly and listen to a friend who has achieved a measure of serenity. Full attention to someone else helps restore our equilibrium and gives us a new perspective on our own lives, so we may see that they don't *have* to be a rat race.

More formal, institutionalized sessions of peace in the company of others (such as religious services, retreats, and the like) are particularly rewarding for certain people.

Or we may simply decide to set out earlier in the day than we used to, so we can move with less hurry. With a little thought, we may be able to work out personal timetables that are less jammed, more flexible, and thus less grinding and goading.

When we do find ourselves up-tight and even frantic, we can ask ourselves occasionally, "Am I really that indispensable?" or "Is this hurry really necessary?" What a relief to find the honest answer is frequently no! And such devices actually serve, in the long run, not only to help us get over our drinking problem and its old ways; they also enable us to become far more productive, because we conserve and channel our energy better. We arrange priorities more sensibly. We learn that many actions once considered vital can be eliminated if they are thoughtfully reexamined. "How much does it really matter?" is a very good question.

Of course, "Easy Does It" gives us no license for procrastination or being late for appointments. There are things that should *not* be put off until tomorrow (and tomorrow and tomorrow)—such as stopping drinking. But there are other things better delayed beyond this 24 hours, to be tackled when we are better equipped to handle them.

Once, an extremely sick and agitated alcoholic called an A.A. office and said she had to have instant help! She was asked whether she could hold on 20 to 30 minutes until someone could be gotten to her.

"Oh no!" she said. "My doctor told me I had to have help right away, immediately, and there isn't a moment to lose."

Then she went on, "And that was day before yesterday!"

Our heart goes out to anyone in that dire condition. We know all too well how it feels. Help did arrive for the excited caller, within the hour, and now she tells the story on herself as an example of what she used to be like. It is almost incredible, when you see how composed yet energetic, how calm but alert she is now.

If a strong inner core of peace, patience, and contentment looks at all desirable to you, it can be had.

Remind yourself once in a while that maybe "Easy Does It" is this day's ideal speed. The change can start right now, remember?

19 Being grateful

One A.A. member recalls that, even during the worst of her drinking career, she never lost her faith. "I had a firm, unshakable belief—in disaster," she explains. "Every morning, almost my first conscious thought was 'Oh, my God, I wonder what new troubles are going to hit me today!'"

When someone knocked at the door, she was sure it was for an unpleasant reason. She confidently expected only bills and other bad news in the mail. And if the telephone rang, she sighed in anticipation of dreary tidings.

Such an enormous expenditure of energy in negative speculations is familiar to many of us; we remember the dark cast of mind that prevailed during the active stage of our own alcoholism. Some of it, to be sure, may have been simply a pharmacological effect of alcohol, which is a depressant drug. When we get the last molecules of alcohol out of the system, a lot of the gloom disappears along with it.

But the habit of thinking in such neurotically depressed ways can stay with some of us, we have found, until we learn to spot it and carefully root it out.

This is no prescription for mindless Pollyanna-ism. We do not pretend that hardships are meaningless, nor deny that everyone has mountains to climb from time to time. Grief really hurts, and so do other kinds of pain.

However, now that we are free of alcohol, we have much more control over our thinking. We have a broader range of thoughts, in minds that are no longer so blurred. The thoughts we choose to spend time on in any given 24 hours can strongly influence the complexion of our feeling for that day—bright and healthy, or murky and disheartened.

Since so much of our thinking used to be intricately associated with our drinking life-style, we have found it worthwhile to look closely at our thinking habits and find different and better ways of using our minds.

The following illustrations may not be an exact fit for you, but even if the words are new, perhaps your emotions will be moved to recognize familiar emotional tunes accompanying them. Some are intentionally exaggerated, to make the point unmistakably clear. Others may, at first glance, look trivial. Scores of us have found, though, that easy little changes are a good starting point for a big strong recovery.

When our favorite toddler falls, bumps her head, and squalls, it's fairly simple to see whether she is seriously hurt or just frightened. Then we have a choice: We can either shriek hysterically because the child got hurt or frightened, and carry on over what could have happened; or we can keep our cool and be comforting, grateful that no serious harm occurred.

When our 90-year-old grandfather, long ill and unhappy, finally dies, we again have a choice. We can insist that the only thing to do is rage in grief and anger at the surprise of it, or wallow in guilt—and perhaps drink in either case. Or we can, besides being sad, remember that he did have a long, often good and happy life; that we did try to be good to him and assure him of our continuing love; and that his suffering and unhappiness are now over. It is doubtful that he would appreciate our using his passing as an excuse to get drunk and endanger our health.

When we finally get to visit a place long dreamed of, we can concentrate on the inconveniences of our lodging and the weather, the passing of the good old days, and the fact that we have only a few days or weeks to spare. Or we can be grateful that we finally got there at all, and keep adding to a mental list of the delights we can find if we look for them.

We can watch out for a tendency to say, "Yes, but—" in response to any optimistic, complimentary, or positive statement. A friend's good luck or his youthful appearance, or a celebrity's plug for a charity may tempt us to say sourly, "Yes, but—" But . . . does this thinking habit help anyone—including ourselves? Can't we let something good simply be? Can't we just be pleased about it, rather than trying to downgrade it?

Those who try to quit smoking realize two possibilities are open: (1) continual moaning about how hard it is, "This time it won't work, either," and "See, damn it, I just lit another one"; or (2) enjoying a deep smoke-free breath when we think of it, being glad an hour has passed without a drag, and, even when a cigarette is unconsciously started, congratulating ourselves for putting it out without smoking it down to a stub.

If one of us wins only $500 in a sweepstakes that has a $50,000 top prize, the sensible mood is easy to pick out. It is *not* bitterness at losing the biggest pot.

We continually find opportunities to make similar considered choices, and our experience convinces us that feeling gratitude is far more wholesome, makes staying sober much easier. It will come as a pleasant surprise to discover that it is not difficult to develop the habit of gratitude if we just make some effort.

Many of us were reluctant to try. But the results, we have to admit, did speak for themselves. It may sting at first to bite the cynical comment from the tip of our tongue. We may have to swallow twice before getting out a mildly positive remark of the type we called saccharine during our drinking life. But it soon comes easier, and can become a strong and comfortable force in our recovery. Life was meant to be enjoyed, and we mean to enjoy it.

Riffling back through the memories of our drinking past, some of us spot another manifestation of negativism. But it, too, is a type of behavior many have learned to change, and the change in our actions has also brought better attitudes and an improvement in our feelings.

For some reason, we spent a lot of time thinking or noting or talking about how wrong or mistaken so many *other* people persistently were. (Whether they really were or not is irrelevant to the welcome change in our own feelings now.) For some, the change begins with a tentative willingness to wait and see, to accept for a moment the hypothesis that the other person just possibly might be right. Before rushing to judgment, we suspend our own argument, listen carefully, and watch for the outcome.

It may, or may not, prove us to be in the wrong. That is not the important issue here. Whichever way the chips fall, we have at least temporarily freed ourselves from our driving need to be always right, or one-up. We have found that a sincere "I don't know" can be rejuvenating. Saying, "I'm wrong, you're right" is invigorating when we are sufficiently at ease with ourselves not to be bothered about actually being in the wrong. We are left feeling relaxed and thankful that we can be open to new ideas. The finest scientists are always alert to new evidence which may prove their own theories wrong, so they can discard any false notions and move closer to the ultimate truth they are seeking.

When we achieve a similar openness, we find our instant negativism has begun to evaporate. Perhaps an illustration can clarify the relationship between the desire to be always right (the negativism of seeing almost everyone else as wrong), and the freedom to be wrong ourselves—to grasp and use new ideas and other help for staying sober.

Many of us, when drinking, were deeply sure for years that our own drinking was harmless. We were not necessarily smart-alecky about it, but when we heard a clergyman, a psychiatrist, or an A.A. member talk about alcoholism, we were quick to observe that *our* drinking was different, that *we* did not need to do any of the things those people suggested. Or even if we could admit that we were having a bit of trouble with our drinking, we were sure we could lick it on our own. Thus we shut the door against new information and help. And behind that door our drinking went on, of course.

Our troubles had to be pretty dire, and we had to begin to feel pretty hopeless before we could open up a little bit and let in some fresh light and help.

For thousands of us, one of the clearest memories which incorporate the wisdom of "being grateful" is our recollection of what we originally thought and said about Alcoholics Anonymous when it first came to our attention:

"It's fine for them, but I'm not that bad, so it isn't for me."

"I've met a couple of former A.A.'s drunk in barrooms. From what they say, I can tell it wouldn't work for me, either."

"I knew a fellow who joined A.A. He turned into a rigid, fanatic, dull, intolerant teetotaler."

"All that God stuff and going to meetings turn me off. Anyhow, I've never been a joiner."

Now, honesty makes us admit that we spent more time concentrating on those negative opinions, and reinforcing our own reasons for drinking, than we spent actually looking into A.A. with an open mind. Our investigation of it was hardly scientific. Rather, it was superficial and pessimistic—a search for things not to like.

We neither talked with many of the sober members, nor read at depth the quantities of literature by and about A.A. If we did not like a few things or people we first encountered in A.A., we gave up. We had tried it, hadn't we? (Remember the man who said he didn't like reading? He had already read a book and didn't like it!)

It is clear now that we could have acted differently. We could have invested some time in searching out things we did like in A.A., ways we could go along with it, statements and ideas we did agree with. We could have been thankful that A.A. welcomes casual visitors, and that we were not required to jump in headlong. We could have been grateful that A.A. has no dues or fees and demands no adherence to any doctrine, rules, or rituals. If some talkative A.A.'s weren't to our taste, we could have been pleased that so many others kept quiet, or spoke more to our liking. We could have kept trying to find out why so many eminent professional experts have endorsed A.A. over and over for many years. It must be doing something right!

Staying sober can boil down to just such a choice, we have learned. We can spend hours thinking of reasons that we want or need or intend to take a drink. Or we can spend the same time listing reasons that drinking is not good for us and abstaining is more healthful, and listing things we can do instead of drinking.

Each of us makes that choice in his or her own way. We are pleased when anyone else chooses to make a decision like ours. But whether you are interested in A.A. or not, we offer good wishes to anyone starting out to stay sober in any way. We keep being grateful that we are free to do it in the ways described here.

20 Remembering your last drunk

That's not a typographical error. The word is "drunk," not "drink," as you'll see.

"A drink" is a term which has awakened pleasurable echoes and anticipations in millions of people for centuries.

Depending on our age, and on the circumstances which surrounded our first experiences with alcohol, we all have various memories and hopes (sometimes, anxieties) aroused by the thought of a cool beer, a bullshot, a gin and tonic, a boilermaker, a sip of wine, or whatever.

Repeatedly, in the early drinking of most people, the anticipations were fully met by the desired drink. And if that happened often enough, we naturally learned to think of "a drink" as a satisfying event—whether it gratified our need to conform to a religious custom, quenched our thirst, graced a social occasion, relaxed us, stimulated us, or gave us any other kind of satisfaction we sought.

It is not difficult for a 55-year-old Finn, for example, when he hears someone suggest a drink, to recall the flush of warmth that a shot of vodka or aquavit brought on a cold day in his youth.

One young woman may instantly visualize an elegant crystal glass of champagne, glamorous surroundings, new clothes, a new lover. Another may think of a pull from a bagged bottle toted by the long-bearded youth in denim at her side while the rock rocks, the strobe lights flash through the sweet smoke, and everybody screams in ecstasy.

One A.A. member says "a drink" makes him almost taste pizza with a brew. A 78-year-old widow among us is inevitably reminded of the sherry eggnogs she began to like at bedtime in a nursing home.

Although perfectly natural, such mental images are now, for us, misleading. Those were the ways some of us *began* to drink, and if that had been the whole truth of our drinking history, it is unlikely that we could have developed much of a drinking problem.

A searching, fearless look at our complete drinking record, however, shows that in the last years and months our drinking never created those perfect, magic moments again, no matter how often we tried for them.

Instead, over and over, we wound up drinking more than that, and landed in some kind of trouble as a result. Maybe it was simply inner discontent, a sneaky feeling that we were drinking too much, but sometimes it was marital squabbles, job problems, serious illness or accidents, or legal or financial worries.

Therefore, when the suggestion of "a drink" comes to us, we now try to remember the *whole* train of consequences of starting with just "a drink." We think the drink all the way through, down to our last miserable drunk and hangover.

A friend who offers us a drink usually means simply that one sociable glass or two. But if we are careful to recall the full suffering of our last drinking episode, we are not deceived by our own long-ago notion of "a drink." The blunt, physiological truth for us, as of today, is that a drink pretty surely means a drunk sooner or later, and that spells trouble.

Drinking *for us* no longer means music and gay laughter and flirtations. It means sickness and sorrow.

One A.A. member puts it this way: "I know now that stopping in for a drink will never again be—for me—simply killing a few minutes and leaving a buck on the bar. In exchange for that drink, what I would plunk down now is my bank account, my family, our home, our car, my job, my sanity, and probably my life. It's too big a price, too big a risk."

He remembers his last drunk, not his first drink.

21 Avoiding dangerous drugs and medications*

Mankind's use of various chemicals to change moods and alter feelings is ancient and widespread. Ethyl alcohol was probably the first of such chemicals, and may have always been the most widely popular drug for this use.

Some drugs have legitimate value and are beneficial when administered by knowledgeable physicians if used solely as directed, and discontinued when they are no longer a medical necessity.

As A.A. members—not physicians—we are certainly not qualified to recommend any medications. Nor are we qualified to advise anyone not to take a prescribed medication.

---

* See also Appendix—excerpt from A.A. Conference-approved pamphlet, "The A.A. Member—Medications and Other Drugs."

What we can do responsibly is to offer only our personal experience.

Drinking became, for many of us, a sort of self-medication. We often drank to feel better and to feel less sick.

And thousands of us used other chemicals, too. We discovered pep pills that seemed to counteract a hangover or relieve our depression (until they let us down, too), sedatives and tranquilizers that could substitute for the alcohol and calm our jitters, bromides and nonprescription pills and elixirs (many of them were called "nonaddictive" or "not habit-forming") that helped us sleep or gave us extra energy or loosened our inhibitions or floated us away on an exquisite surge of bliss.

Potentially, this strong desire, almost a need, for such psychoactive (mind-affecting) mood-changers can be embedded root-deep in anybody who is much of a drinker.

Even if, technically, in pharmacological terms, a drug is not a physiologically addictive one, we can easily get habituated to it and dependent on it, we have repeatedly found. It's as if "addiction proneness" was a condition inside *us*, not a quality of the drug itself. Some of us believe we have become "addictive" people, and our experience gives reinforcing support to that concept.

So we go to great lengths to avoid all street drugs—marijuana, "crank," "downers," "uppers," cocaine, "hash," hallucinogens, "speed" —and even many over-the-counter pills and nostrums, as well as tranquilizers.

Even to those of us who never got hooked on any of them, it is clear that they represent a real potential danger, for we have seen it demonstrated over and over and over again. Drugs will often reawaken the old craving for "oral magic," or some kind of high, or peace. And if we get by with using them once or twice, it oftens seems ever so much easier to pick up a drink.

The Fellowship of Alcoholics Anonymous is not an antidrug or antimarijuana lobby. As a whole, we take no moral or legal position either for or against grass or any other such substance. (Every member of A.A., though, is entitled, like any other adult, to hold any opinion on these matters, and to take any action that seems right to him or to her.)

This is somewhat similar to A.A. members' position—or probably "non-position" is more accurate—on booze and drinking. As a fellowship, we are not antialcohol or against drinking for the millions of people who can use it without causing any harm, either to themselves or to others.

Some (but not all) of us who have been sober a while are quite willing to serve drinks in our homes to our nonalcoholic guests. To drink or not is their right. Not to drink, or to drink if we choose, is equally our right, and we have no quarrel with what other people do. We have generally concluded, for ourselves only, that drinking is not good for us, and we have found ways of living without it which we much prefer to our drunken days.

Not all, but quite a few recovered alcoholics find that their body chemistry has become permanently tolerant to painkilling drugs, so they have to have extra large doses when an analgesic or anesthetic is required for medical purposes.

Some of us report adverse reactions to local anesthetics (such as Novocain) injected by a dentist. At the least, we leave the chair extremely nervous, and the condition may last quite a while, unless we can lie down a bit to let it wear off. (The company of another recovered alcoholic is soothing at such times.)

Other recovered alcoholics report no such adverse reactions. No one has any idea how to predict in which instances such reactions will occur. Anyhow, it is surely wise to tell our doctor, dentist, and hospital anesthesiologist the whole truth about our former drinking (and pill-taking, if any), just as we make sure they know other facts about our health history.

The two following accounts seem to be typical of A.A. members' experiences with psychotropic (mind-affecting) drugs other than alcohol.

One of us, sober almost thirty years, decided he wanted to try pot, which he had never touched before. So he did. He enjoyed the effects and for months was able to use it on social occasions without any problem at all, he felt. Then someone said a small sip of wine made the effect even better, and he tried that, too, without even thinking about his bad history of alcoholism. After all, he was having only one sip of a very light wine.

Within a month, he was drinking heavily and realized he was again in the thrall of acute alcoholism.

We could put a hundred or so dittos under that tale, with only small modifications. It is a pleasure to report that this particular fellow sobered up, also gave up the weed, and has now been totally pot- and booze-free for two years. He is again a happy, active sober alcoholic, enjoying his A.A. life.

Not all who have similarly experimented with marijuana have made it back into sobriety. For some of these A.A. members, whose pot-smoking likewise led them to start drinking again, their original addiction progressed to the point of death.

The other story is that of a young woman, sober ten years, who was hospitalized for serious surgery. Her physician, who was an expert on alcoholism, told her it would be necessary after the surgery to give her a small dose of morphine once or twice for the pain, but he assured her she wouldn't need it any longer after that. This woman had never in her life used anything stronger than one aspirin tablet, for a rare headache.

The second night after the operation, she asked her doctor for one more dose of the morphine. She had already had the two. "Are you in pain?" he asked.

"No," she replied. Then she added in complete innocence, "But I might be later."

When he grinned at her, she realized what she had said, and what it apparently meant. Her mind and body in some way were already craving the drug.

She laughed and did without it, and has had no such desire since. Five years later, she is still sober and healthy. She occasionally tells of the incident at A.A. meetings to illustrate her own belief that a permanent "addiction proneness" persists even during sobriety in anyone who has ever had a drinking problem.

So most of us try to make sure any physician or dentist who serves us understands our personal history accurately, and is sufficiently knowledgeable about alcoholism to understand our risk with medications.

And we are wary of what we take on our own; we steer away from cough syrups with alcohol, codeine, or bromides, and from all those assorted smokes, powders, synthetic painkillers, liquids, and vapors that are sometimes freely handed around by unauthorized pharmacists or amateur anesthesiologists.

Why take a chance?

It is not at all difficult, we find, to skip such risky brushes with disaster—purely on grounds of health, not of morality. Through Alcoholics Anonymous, we have found a drug-free way of life which, to us, is far more satisfying than any we ever experienced with mood-changing substances.

The chemical "magic" we felt from alcohol (or substitutes for it) was all locked within our own heads, anyhow. Nobody else could share the pleasant sensations inside us. Now, we enjoy sharing with one another in A.A.—or with anybody outside A.A.—our natural, undoped happiness.

In time, the nervous system becomes healthy and thoroughly conditioned to the absence of mood-changing drugs, such as firewater. When we feel more comfortable without chemical substances than we felt while we were dependent on them, we come to accept and trust our normal feelings, whether high or low.

Then we have the strength to make healthful, independent decisions, relying less on impulse or the chemically triggered urge for immediate satisfaction. We can see and consider more aspects of a situation than before, can delay gratification for the sake of more enduring, long-term benefits, and can better weigh, not only our own welfare, but also that of others we care for.

Chemical substitutes for life simply do not interest us any more, now that we know what genuine living is.

22 Eliminating self-pity

This emotion is so ugly that no one in his or her right mind wants to admit feeling it. Even when sober, many of us remain clever at hiding from ourselves the fact that we are astew in a mess of self-pity. We do not like at all being told that it shows, and we are sharp at arguing that we are experiencing some other emotion—not that loathsome poor-me-ism. Or we can, in a second, find a baker's dozen of perfectly legitimate reasons for feeling somewhat sorry for ourselves.

Hanging over us long after detoxification is the comfortably familiar feeling of suffering. Self-pity is an enticing swamp. Sinking into it takes so much less effort than hope, or faith, or just plain moving.

Alcoholics are not unique in this. Everyone who can recall a childhood pain or illness can probably remember, too, the relief of crying over how bad we felt, and the somewhat perverse satisfaction of rejecting all comforting. Almost any human being, at times, can deeply empathize with the childish whine of "Leave me alone!"

One form self-pity takes in some of us when we first get sober is: "Poor me! Why can't I drink like everybody else?" *(Everybody?)* "Why does this have to happen to *me?* Why do *I* have to be an alcoholic? Why *me*?"

Such thinking is a great ticket to a barroom, but that's about all. Crying over that unanswerable question is like weeping because we were born in this era, not another, or on this planet, rather than in some other galaxy.

Of course, it isn't just "me" at all, we discover when we begin to meet recovered alcoholics from all over the world.

Later on, we realize we have begun to make our peace with that question. When we really hit our stride in an enjoyable recovery, we may either find an answer or simply lose interest in the search. You'll know when that happens to you. Many of us believe we have figured out the likely reasons for our own alcoholism. But even if we haven't, there remains the much more important need to accept the fact that we cannot drink, and to act on it. Sitting in our own pool of tears is not a very effective action.

Some people show real zeal for pressing salt into their own wounds. A ferocious proficiency at that useless game often survives from our drinking days.

We can also display a weird flair for expanding a minor annoyance into a whole universe of gloom. When the mail brings a whopping telephone bill—just one—we bemoan our *constantly* being in debt, and declare it will never, *never* end. When a soufflé falls, we say it proves that we never could and never will do anything right. When the new car arrives, we say to somebody, "With my luck, it'll be a . . ."

If you finished that statement with the name of a sour citrus, you're in our club.

It's as if we carried on our back a large duffel bag stuffed with unpleasant memories, such as childhood hurts and rejections. Twenty, even forty years later, there occurs a small setback only slightly similar to an old one in the bag. That is our cue to sit down, unshoulder the bag, and pull out and lovingly caress, one at a time, every old hurt and putdown of the past. With total emotional recall, we then relive each of them vividly, flushing with shame at childhood embarrassments, grinding our teeth on old angers, rewording old quarrels, shivering with nearly forgotten fear, or maybe blinking away a tear or two over a long-gone disappointment in love.

Those are fairly extreme cases of unadulterated self-pity, but not beyond recognition by anybody who has ever had, seen, or wanted to go on a crying jag. Its essence is total self-absorption. We can get so stridently concerned about me-me-me that we lose touch with virtually everyone else. It's not easy to put up with anyone who acts that way, except a sick infant. So when we get into the poor-me bog, we try to hide it, particularly from ourselves. But that's no way to get out of it.

Instead, we need to pull out of our self-absorption, stand back, and take a good, honest look at ourselves. Once we recognize self-pity for what it is, we can start to do something about it other than drink.

Friends can be a great help if they're close enough that we can talk openly with each other. They can hear the false note in our song of sorrow and call us on it. Or we ourselves may hear it; we begin to get our true feelings sorted out by the simple means of expressing them aloud.

Another excellent weapon is humor. Some of the biggest belly laughs at A.A. meetings erupt when a member describes his or her own latest orgy of self-pity, and we listeners find ourselves looking into a fun-house mirror. There we are—grown men and women tangled up in the emotional diaper of an infant. It may be a shock, but the shared laughter takes a lot of the pain out of it, and the final effect is salutary.

When we catch self-pity starting, we also can take action against it with instant bookkeeping. For every entry of misery on the debit side, we find a blessing we can mark on the credit side. What health we have, what illnesses we don't have, what friends we have loved, the sunny weather, a good meal a-coming, limbs intact, kindnesses shown and received, a sober 24 hours, a good hour's work, a good book to read, and many other items can be totaled up to outbalance the debit entries that cause self-pity.

We can use the same method to combat the holiday blues, which are sung not only by alcoholics. Christmas and New Year's, birthdays, and anniversaries throw many other people into the morass of self-pity. In A.A., we can learn to recognize the old inclination to concentrate on nostalgic sadness, or to keep up a litany of who is gone, who neglects us now, and how little we can give in comparison to rich people. Instead, we add up the other side of the ledger, in gratitude for health, for loved ones who *are* around, and for our ability to give love, now that we live in sobriety. And again, the balance comes out on the credit side.

23 Seeking professional help

Probably every recovered alcoholic has needed and sought professional help of the sort A.A. does not provide. For instance, the first two A.A. members, its co-founders, needed and got help from physicians, hospitals, and clergymen.

Once we have started staying sober, a lot of our problems seem to disappear. But certain matters remain, or arise, which do require expert professional attention, such as that of an obstetrician, a chiropodist, a lawyer, a chest expert, a dentist, a dermatologist, or a psychological counselor of some kind.

Since A.A. does not furnish such services, we rely on the professional community for job-getting or vocational guidance, advice on domestic relations, counseling on psychiatric problems, and many other needs. A.A. does not give financial assistance, food, clothing, or shelter to problem drinkers. But there are good professional agencies and facilities particularly happy to help out an alcoholic who is sincerely trying to stay sober.

One's need for a helping hand is no sign of weakness and no cause for shame. "Pride" that prevents one's taking an encouraging boost from a professional helper is phony. It is nothing but vanity, and an obstacle to recovery. The more mature one becomes, the more willing one is to use the best possible advice and help.

Examining "case histories" of recovered alcoholics, we can see clearly that all of us have profited, at one time or another, from the specialized services of psychiatrists and other physicians, nurses, counselors, social workers, lawyers, clergymen, or other professional people. The basic A.A. textbook, "Alcoholics Anonymous," specifically recommends (on page 74) seeking out such help. Fortunately, we have found no conflict between A.A. ideas and the good advice of a professional with expert understanding of alcoholism.

We do not deny that alcoholics have had many unfortunate experiences with some professional men and women. But nonalcoholics, since there are more of them, have had even more such experiences. The absolutely perfect doctor, pastor, or lawyer, who never makes a mistake, has not come along yet. And as long as there are sick people in the world, it is likely that the time will never come when no errors are ever committed in dealing with illness.

In fairness, we have to confess that problem drinkers are not exactly the easiest people to help. We sometimes lie. We disobey instructions. And when we get well, we blame the doctor for not undoing sooner the damage we spent weeks, months, or years wreaking on ourselves. Not all of us paid our bills promptly. And, time after time, we did our best to sabotage good care and advice, to put the professional person "in the wrong." It was a cheap, false win, since in the end it was we who suffered the consequences.

Some of us are now aware that our behavior prevented our getting the good advice or care we really needed. One way of explaining our contrary conduct is to say that it was dictated by our illness. Alcohol is cunning and baffling. It can force anyone in its chains to behave in a self-destructive manner, against his or her own better judgment and true desires. We did not plan willfully to foul up our own health; our addiction to alcohol was simply protecting itself against any inroads by health agents.

If we now find ourselves sober but still trying to second-guess the really expert professionals, it can be taken as a warning signal. Is active alcoholism trying to sneak its way back into us?

In some instances, the conflicting opinions and recommendations of other recovering alcoholics can make it hard for a newcomer seeking

good professional help. Just as nearly every person has a favorite antidote for a hangover or remedy for the common cold, so nearly everyone we know has favorite and unfavorite doctors.

Of course, it is wise to draw on the large bank of accumulated wisdom of alcoholics already well along in recovery. But what works for
others isn't always necessarily what will work for you. Each of us has
to accept final responsibility for his or her own action or inaction. It is
up to each individual.

After you have examined the various possibilities, consulted with
friends, and considered the pros and cons, the decision to get and use
professional help is ultimately your own. To take or not to take disulfi-
ram (Antabuse), to go into psychotherapy, to go back to school or
change jobs, to have an operation, to go on a diet, to quit smoking, to
take or disregard your lawyer's advice about your taxes—these are all
your own decisions. We respect your right to make them—and to
change your mind when developments so warrant.

Naturally, not all medical, psychological, or other scientific experts
see exactly eye-to-eye with us on everything in this booklet. That's perfectly okay. How could they? They have not had the personal, firsthand
experience we have had with alcoholism, and very few of them see as
many problem drinkers for as long as we do. Nor have we had the professional education and discipline which prepared them for their duties.

This is not to say that they are right and we are wrong, or vice versa.
We and they have entirely different roles and responsibilities in helping problem drinkers.

May you have the same good fortune in these regards that so many
of us have had. Hundreds of thousands of us are deeply grateful to the
countless professional men and women who helped us, or tried to.

24 Steering clear of emotional entanglements

Falling in love with your doctor or nurse or a fellow patient is an old
romantic story. Recovering alcoholics are susceptible to the same
fever. In fact, alcoholism does not seem to bring immunity from any
known human condition.

Sorrow is born in the hasty heart, an old saw goes. Other troubles,
including an alcoholic bout, can be, too.

During our days of bottles, cans, and glasses, many of us spent a lot of time concerned about intimate personal ties. Whether we wanted temporary partnerships or a long-term "meaningful relationship," we were often preoccupied with our deep involvement—or noninvolvement—with other people.

A great many of us blamed our drinking on lack of affection, saw ourselves as constantly in search of love, drinking as we prowled from bar to party. Others of us apparently had all the emotional ties we needed or wanted, but drank anyhow. Either way, alcohol certainly did not ripen our comprehension of mature love, nor our ability to enter into and handle it if it did come our way. Rather, our drinking lives left our emotional selves pinched, scraped, bent, and bruised, if not pretty firmly warped.

So, as our experience shows, the first nondrinking days are likely to be periods of great emotional vulnerability. Is this an extended pharmacological effect of the drinking? Is it a natural state for anyone recuperating from a long and severe illness? Or does it indicate a deep flaw in the personality? The answer doesn't matter at first. Whatever the cause, the condition is one we have to watch out for, because it can tempt us to drink faster than the eye, head, or heart can realize.

We have seen such relapses happen in several ways. In the early relief and delight of getting well, we can whip up enormous crushes on new people we meet, both in A.A. and outside it, especially when they show genuine interest in us, or seem to gaze up at us in admiration. The giddy rapture this can bring makes us highly susceptible to a drink.

An emotional opposite can also be the case. We may seem so numb that we are almost immune to affection for a while after stopping drinking. (Clinicians tell us it is common for people to have no interest or very much ability in sex for many months after stopping drinking—but that problem straightens itself out beautifully as health returns. We know!) Until we are assured that the numbness will pass, going back to drinking appears an attractive "remedy," which leads to even worse trouble.

Our shaky emotional condition also affects our feelings toward old friends and family. For many of us, these relationships seem to heal promptly as we pursue recovery. For others, there arrives a period of touchiness at home; now that we're sober, we have to sort out how we actually feel about spouse, children, siblings, parents, or neighbors, then reexamine our behavior. Fellow workers, clients, employees, or employers also require such attention.

(Often, our drinking has had a severe emotional impact on those closest to us, and they, too, may need help in recovering. They may turn to Al-Anon Family Groups and Alateen [see your telephone directory].

Although these fellowships are not officially connected with A.A., they are very similar, and they help nonalcoholic relatives and friends to live more comfortably with knowledge about us and our condition.)

Over the years, we have become strongly convinced that almost no important decisions should be arrived at early in our sobriety, unless they cannot possibly be delayed. This caution particularly applies to decisions about people, decisions with high emotional potential. The first, uncertain weeks of sobriety are no time to rush into major life changes.

Another caution: Tying our sobriety to someone we are emotionally involved with proves flatly disastrous. "I'll stay sober if so-and-so does this or that" puts an unhealthy condition on our recovery. We have to stay sober for ourselves, no matter what other people do or fail to do.

We should remember, too, that intense dislike also is an emotional entanglement, often a reversal of past love. We need to cool *any* overboard feeling, lest it flip us back into the drink.

It is easy to consider yourself an exception to this generalization. Newly sober, you may earnestly believe that you have at long last found *real* love—or that your present attitude of dislike, persisting even into sobriety, means there always was something fundamentally wrong about the relationship. In either instance, you *may* be right—but just now, it's wise to wait and see whether your attitude will change.

Again and again, we have seen such feelings change dramatically in only a few months of sobriety. So, using "First Things First," we have found it helpful to concentrate first on sobriety alone, steering clear of *any* risky emotional entanglements.

Immature or premature liaisons are crippling to recovery. Only after we have had time to mature somewhat beyond merely not drinking are we equipped to relate maturely to other people.

When our sobriety has a foundation firm enough to withstand stress, *then* we are ready to work through and straighten out other aspects of our lives.

25 Getting out of the 'if' trap

Emotional entanglements with people are not the only way we can get our sobriety dangerously hooked to something extraneous. Some of us have a tendency to put other conditions on our sobriety, without intending to.

One A.A. member says, "We drunks* are very 'iffy' people. During our drinking days, we were often full of ifs, as well as liquor. A lot of our day-dreams started out, *'If* only...' And we were continually saying to our-selves that we wouldn't have gotten drunk *if* something or other hadn't happened, or that we wouldn't have any drinking problem at all *if* only..."

We all followed up that last "if" with our own explanations (excuses?) for our drinking. Each of us thought: I wouldn't be drinking this way...

If it wasn't for my wife (or husband or lover)...if I just had more money and not so many debts...if it wasn't for all these family prob-lems...if I wasn't under so much pressure...if I had a better job or a better place to live...if people understood me...if the state of the world wasn't so lousy...if human beings were kinder, more considerate, more honest...if everybody else didn't expect me to drink...if it wasn't for the war (any war)...and on and on and on.

Looking back at this kind of thinking and our resultant behavior, we see now that we were really letting circumstances outside ourselves control much of our lives.

When we first stop drinking, a lot of those circumstances recede to their proper places in our minds. At the personal level, many of them really clear up as soon as we start staying sober, and we begin to see what we may be able to do about the others some day. Meanwhile, our life is much, much better sober, no matter what else may be going on.

But then, after a sober while, for some of us there comes a time when—plop!—a new discovery slaps us in the face. That same old "iffy" thinking habit of our tippling days has, without our seeing it, attached itself to not drinking. Unconsciously, we have placed condi-tions on our sobriety. We have begun to think sobriety is just fine—*if* everything goes well, or *if* nothing goes askew.

In effect, we are ignoring the biochemical, unchangeable nature of our ailment. Alcoholism respects no ifs. It does not go away, not for a week, for a day, or even for an hour, leaving us nonalcoholic and able to drink again on some special occasion or for some extraordinary rea-son—not even if it is a once-in-a-lifetime celebration, or if a big sorrow hits us, or if it rains in Spain or the stars fall on Alabama. Alcoholism is for us unconditional, with no dispensations available at any price.

It may take a little while to get that knowledge into the marrow of our bones. And we sometimes do not recognize the conditions we have

---

* Some of us A.A.'s refer to ourselves as "drunks," no matter how long we have been sober. Others prefer "alcoholics." There are good reasons for both terms. "Drunks" is lighthearted, tends to keep the ego down to size, and reminds us of our proneness to drinking. "Alcoholics" is equally honest, but more dignified and more in keeping with the now widely accepted idea that alcoholism is a perfectly respectable illness, not just willful self-indulgence.

unconsciously attached to our recovery until something goes wrong through no fault of ours. Then—whammy!—there it is. We had not counted on *this* happening.

The thought of a drink is natural in the face of a shocking disappointment. If we don't get the raise, promotion, or job we counted on, or if our love life goes awry, or if somebody mistreats us, then we can see that maybe all along we have been banking on circumstances to help us want to stay sober.

Somewhere, buried in a hidden convolution of our gray matter, we had a tiny reservation—a condition on our sobriety. And it was just waiting to pounce. We were going along thinking, "Yep, sobriety is great, and I intend to keep at it." We didn't even hear the whispered reservation: "That is, *if* everything goes my way."

Those ifs we cannot afford. We have to stay sober no matter how life treats us, no matter whether nonalcoholics appreciate our sobriety or not. We have to keep our sobriety independent of everything else, not entangled with any people, and not hedged in by any possible cop-outs or conditions.

Over and over, we have found we cannot stay sober long just for the sake of wife, husband, children, lover, parents, other relative, or friend, nor for the sake of a job, nor to please a boss (or doctor or judge or creditor)—not for *anyone* other than ourselves.

Tying up our sobriety to *any* person (even another recovered alcoholic) or to *any* circumstance is foolish and dangerous. When we think, "I'll stay sober *if*—" or "I won't drink because of—" (fill in any circumstance other than our own desire to be well, for health's own sake), we unwittingly set ourselves up to drink when the condition or person or circumstance changes. And any of these may change at any moment.

Independent, unaffiliated with anything else, our sobriety can grow strong enough to enable us to cope with anything—and everybody. And, as you'll see, we start liking *that* feeling, too.

26 Being wary of drinking occasions

We have worked out many ways of handling occasions when other people are drinking, so that we may enjoy these occasions without drinking.

Back on page 21, we talked about whether to keep liquor or other alcoholic beverages in the house when we decide to stop drinking. In that discussion, we acknowledged that we live in a society where most people drink, and we cannot realistically expect that fact to change. Throughout the rest of our lives, there will be drinking occasions. Chances are, every day we will see people drinking, see drinking places, see and hear dozens of advertisements urging us to drink.

We cannot insulate ourselves against all such suggestions, and it is futile to bemoan that fact. Nor do we have any need or wish to deprive other people of drinking. We have also found that we do not have to forgo the pleasure of being with companions who drink. Although it makes sense to spend more time with nondrinkers than with drinkers when we *first* start staying sober, we have no wish to withdraw from the world forever just because so many people drink. Those who cannot eat fish or nuts or pork or strawberries don't crawl into caves. Why should we?

Do we go into bars, or into restaurants or clubs where liquor is served?

Yes—after a few weeks or months, when we have a *legitimate* reason to be there. If we have time to kill while waiting for friends, we do not choose to spend it perched on a barstool, swilling a cola. But if a business or social event occurs in such a place, we attend and participate in all but the drinking.

For the first nondrinking months, it's probably a healthy idea to stay away from our old drinking buddies and haunts, and to find reasonable excuses for skipping parties where drinking will be a major entertainment. It seems especially important to stay away from such affairs if we feel nervous about them.

But, sooner or later, there comes the time when a family or business obligation or a friendship makes us feel compelled to go—or perhaps we just want to go. We have developed a number of ways to render such occasions easy for us to take, even though we abstain. Now, we are talking primarily about the big cocktail party or the fairly large but informal dinner-with-drinks evening.

If the host or hostess is an old friend we can level with, sometimes it helps to tell him or her in advance that we are not drinking right now. We do not ask for any special treatment, of course. But it's reassuring to know there will be at least one person present who is completely sympathetic to our efforts to get over a drinking problem. Sometimes, we can take with us a more experienced nondrinker, or at least a companion who knows we are abstaining and realizes how important it is to us.

It is also beneficial, before you go, to talk with another recovered alcoholic or with someone else on your side, who is rooting for your health and fully understands the pressure you'll be under. Arrange to call back later and tell how it went. Another recovered alcoholic would appreciate such a call very much. Believe us! We A.A.'s get a thrill from every such message.

It is a very good idea to eat a sandwich or other snack before going to a party, even if you know food will be served later. Something nourishing in the stomach, as we've already said, takes the edge off many trying situations. (And you might carry along a small packet of your favorite mints or a dietetic substitute.) This is even more important when you are headed for a party at which there are likely to be some long heavy-drinking hours before food appears.

When you know that will be the schedule, you may prefer to skip the first hour or so of the drinking and arrive only shortly before dinner is served. Many of us do this. Then, if there is going to be a long drunk evening after eating, we have found it is also easy to leave early. The very few who do notice our slipping away, we have discovered, hardly mind our departure at all. They are too busy drinking, or whatever.

Upon arriving at such a party, it is usually best to bead straight for the bar and get a glass of ginger ale or other soda. No one knows whether it is an alcoholic drink or not. Then we can walk about socializing, glass in band, without feeling conspicuous.

This experience was quite revealing to many of us when we first had it. We discovered to our surprise that (1) other people's drinking is not what we thought it was, and (2) very, very few people observe, or care, whether or not we drink alcohol. (Some exceptions to the latter are likely to be loving friends or relatives, who are usually glad to see us doing something about our drinking.)

Many of us used to say, and believe, that "everybody" drinks, and we could argue that we did not drink a lot more than the other drinkers we knew. To tell the truth, as our drinking went on over the years, many of us tended to associate less and less with nondrinkers, so of course it seemed to us that "everybody"—certainly everybody we saw—drank.

Now, sober, when we see "everybody," it is a revelation to find that not all of them do drink, and that many of the others drink much less than we had supposed.

Anticipating occasions like these, the newly sober alcoholic wonders what to answer if drinking friends and relatives say such things as:

"Come have a drink."

"What are you drinking?"

"Why, you *can't* be an alcoholic!"

"Don't you drink?"

"Just one won't hurt."

"Why aren't you drinking?"… and the like.

To our relief, we found that these questions come up less often than we expected, and our answers seem to have much less importance than we thought they would have. Our not drinking creates less of a stir than we feared it would.

There is one exception. Once in a while, a really heavy drinker will get pretty pushy about our not drinking. Most of us come to believe that such an attitude is very suspicious. Civilized, polite people simply do not carry on that much about what other people choose to drink or eat, or not to drink or eat, unless they have some hang-up of their own, do they? We find it curious that anyone should try to get a person to drink who does not care to; and we especially wonder why anybody wants a person with a record of drinking-related problems to try to drink again.

We learn to steer clear of such people. If they do indeed have their own hang-up to contend with, we wish them well. But we need not defend our choices to them or to anyone else. And we do not argue with them, or try to change their minds. Again, our attitude is "Live and Let Live."

But back to those questions asked politely and casually by well-meaning friends and relatives, and our answers to them. There are probably as many good ways to handle these situations as there are nondrinkers, and your own intelligence will lead you to the one that works best and is most comfortable for you.

However, the outlines of several different successful methods have emerged from the years of accumulated experience of Alcoholics Anonymous. The past has banked its wisdom, and it is foolish not to draw on it.

Great numbers of us (but not all) believe that the sooner we establish the truth with our acquaintances, the better it is for us. We do not have to keep up any pretenses, and most good people appreciate our honesty and encourage our efforts to stay free of our addiction. Saying aloud to other people that we do not drink helps greatly to strengthen our own determination to stay sober. And there may be a by-product: Occasionally, we find that making such a statement encourages someone else present who also needs or wants not to drink.

Therefore, many of us do not hesitate, when it is appropriate, to say, "I'm not drinking now."

"I'm not drinking today (or this week)" or simply "No, thanks" or a straightforward "I don't care for any" often satisfies the questioner.

If we feel the need to explain any further, we try to do it without lying, and in a way that other people can rapidly understand and accept. For instance, there are old standbys like "Health reasons," "I'm on a diet," and "Doctor's orders." Most of us, at one time or another, have been given or have read some such advice by a physician.

"I've had my share," "Had all I can handle," and "Found out it doesn't agree with me" are also truthful.

While we A.A.'s do not use, among ourselves, the expression "on the wagon," it is something most people certainly understand and respect, as long as we do not urge others to abstain.

Although we certainly cannot recommend untruthfulness, because of the way it makes *us* feel, occasionally some of us in desperation have resorted to the "little white lie," one of those small fibs believed to be harmless and sometimes described as necessary lubrication for the smooth operation of society.

When we have to fall back on manufactured, murmured excuses for not drinking, we try to reach for one that is not too far-fetched. "I have a mysterious disease" or "I'm on some medication" might shut people up, but more likely would evoke extra questions.

Usually, "I'm allergic to it" seems acceptable. Technically, in strictly scientific terms, alcoholism is not a true allergy, the experts now inform us. However, "allergy" is a pretty good figure of speech to describe our condition; if we imbibe the stuff, regrettable consequences certainly do follow.

When we do offer such a statement, it usually produces the desired response. That is, people accept the fact that we are not going to drink right now, and stop questioning us about it.

When we're asked what we'd like to drink, it seems courteous and sensible to ask for and promptly accept something nonalcoholic, whether or not it is our particular favorite. Most of us take any soft drink, fruit or vegetable juice, or other nontoxic beverage that is easily available. (We can pretend to sip it if we really are not fond of it or not thirsty.) This puts us more at ease, and also relieves the hospitable host or hostess who is a compulsive glass-filler and seems genuinely uncomfortable if a guest is not swallowing.

The formal seated banquet, with an array of wineglasses, is no particular problem. Simply turning a wineglass upside down is signal enough for a good waiter or wine steward, even in the wine-drinking countries of Europe. Some of us ask for seltzer or a sparkling mineral water. And when a toast is proposed, almost no one pays attention to us as long as we lift *some* glass, with something in it. After all, isn't it the symbolic pledge of friendship that makes a toast real, not the presence of a drug (ethyl alcohol) in the glass or loving cup?

No one is under any obligation to answer rude or personal questions; so, in the rare event that one is raised, we ignore it or finesse it or change the subject. If that happens to you, remember there are hundreds of thousands of us now recovered from alcoholism who are on your side and understand perfectly what you are undergoing and why you do it, even if no one else seems to. Even if we are not present, in our hearts we are with you, and you can assure yourself that you have our very good wishes.

One other kind of incident has happened to some of us. It is not especially serious or dangerous, but maybe our telling about it will help prevent your being upset if it comes up in your life. Once in a while, a good-hearted, well-intentioned friend or family member inadvertently overdoes the concern about our recovery and, meaning only to help us, may embarrass us if we are not poised enough to handle the situation.

For instance, the nonalcoholic spouse, understandably fearing that we may drink again and trying too hard to protect us, will blurt out, "So-and-so has stopped drinking." Or a solicitous friend may thoughtlessly call attention to our not drinking by pointing to the one glass of tomato juice on a tray of drinks and saying, "That's for you."

It is good of them to want to help us, and we try to concentrate on their desire to be kind. In all fairness, they cannot be expected to understand instantly how we feel. Some of us can't even sort out how we actually do feel until we have some nondrinking time and the self-conscious phase has passed.

Naturally, we prefer to be allowed to make our own choices, discreetly and privately, without a public show. But getting touchy about what other people say or do hurts no one but ourselves. It is better to try to grin and bear it, getting past the moment somehow. It is usually over in less than five minutes. Maybe later, when we feel calm, we can quietly explain that we genuinely appreciate the concern, but would feel better if allowed to make our own "excuses." We might add that we'd like to practice protecting ourselves in social situations, so that the other person need not worry when we're on our own.

After even more time has passed, many of us reach a stage of real comfort about ourselves and drinking; we are relaxed enough to tell the exact truth—that we are "recovered alcoholics," or that we are in A.A.

This face-to-face, confidential revelation about ourselves in no way conflicts with A.A.'s tradition of anonymity, which suggests that we not reveal those facts about anyone *except* ourselves, and that we not make such announcements for publication or on broadcasts.

When we can tell this, with ease, about ourselves, it shows that we have nothing to hide, and that we are not ashamed to be recovering from an illness. It helps to increase our self-respect. Such statements chip away at the cruel old stigma unfairly placed by ignorant people on victims of our malady, and help to replace old, stereotyped notions of "an alcoholic" with more accurate perceptions.

Incidentally, such a statement very often induces someone else who wants to get over a drinking problem to try to seek aid, too.

Just one more thing about this matter of drinking occasions. Many of us have had the guts, if pressure to drink really got unpleasantly strong, simply to make an excuse and leave, no matter what other people may think. After all, our life is at stake. We simply have to take whatever steps are necessary to preserve our own health. Other people's reactions are *their* problem, not ours.

27 Letting go of old ideas

The ideas that got so deeply embedded in our lives during drinking do not all disappear quickly, as if by magic, the moment we start keeping the plug in the jug. Our days of wine and "Sweet Adeline" may be gone, but the malady lingers on.

So we have found it therapeutic to nip off many old ideas that start to sprout up again. And they do, over and over.

What we try to achieve is a feeling of being relaxed and freed from the bonds of our old thinking. Many of our former habits of thought, and the ideas they produced, limit our freedom. They just weigh us down and are of no use—so it turns out when we look them over with a fresh eye. We don't *have* to hang on to them any longer unless, upon examination, they prove valid and still truly fruitful.

We can now measure the present-day usefulness and truthfulness of a thought against a highly specific standard. We can say to ourselves, "Now, that is exactly what I used to think, in the drinking days. Does that kind of thinking help me stay sober? Is it good enough for me *today*?"

Many of our old ideas—especially those about alcohol, about drinking, about getting drunk, and about alcoholism (or problem drinking, if you prefer that term)—prove either worthless or actually self-destructive for us, and it is a great relief to get rid of them. Maybe a few examples will suffice to illustrate our willingness to throw out our old, useless ideas.

For many of us as teen-agers, drinking was a way of proving that we were no longer children, or that we were manly, or sophisticated and wise, or tough enough to defy parents and other authorities. In many minds, drinking is closely tied in with romance, sex, and music, or with business success, wine snobbery, and jet-set luxury. If one is taught anything about drinking at school, it is often about dangers to health and the likelihood of losing a driver's license—not much else. And many people are still convinced that any drinking at all is immoral, leading straight to crime, suffering, disgrace, and death. Whatever our feelings may have been about drinking, positive or negative, they were often strong and more emotional than rational.

Or our attitudes toward drinking may have been merely automatic, an unthinking acceptance of other people's opinions. To many, drinking is an essential part of social occasions—a harmless, convivial pastime done in certain places among friends at specific times. Others view drinking as a necessary accompaniment to eating. But now we ask ourselves: *Is* it actually impossible to enjoy friendship or food without drinking? Did our own way of drinking improve our social relationships? Did it heighten our appreciation of good food?

The idea of getting drunk produces reactions even more extreme, pro or con. Getting tight is likely to be seen only as fun, or only as disgraceful. The very idea is repugnant to many people, on various grounds. To some of us, it was a desirable state, not only because it was expected of us by others and we liked the feeling, but also because it was a condition made light of by glamorous celebrities. Some people are intolerant of those who never get drunk at all; others are scornful of those who get *too* drunk. Modern-day health findings so far have had little influence on such attitudes.

When we first heard the word "alcoholic," most of us associated it exclusively with older, unkempt, shaky, or unpleasant men we saw panhandling or passed out on skid rows. Well-informed people are now aware that such an idea is rubbish.

Nevertheless, a residue of our ancient, muddy notions clung to many of us during our first attempts at sobriety. They blurred our vision and made it difficult to see the truth. But we finally became willing to entertain the thought that—just possibly—some of those ideas could be a bit erroneous, or at least no longer reflected accurately our own personal experience.

When we could persuade ourselves to look at that experience honestly and to listen to ideas other than our own, we became open to a big array of information we had not examined carefully before.

For instance, we could look at the scientific description: Alcohol is a drug that alters consciousness, not just a tasty thirst-quencher. The drug is found, we learned, not only in beverages, but also in some foods and medicines. And now, almost every day, we read or hear of a discovery that this particular drug does one more kind of physical damage (to the heart, the blood, the stomach, the liver, the mouth, the brain, etc.) not suspected before.

Pharmacologists and other addictions experts now say that alcohol is not to be considered totally safe and harmless, whether used as beverage, stimulant, sedative, tonic, or tranquilizer. But it does not, of itself, necessarily lead straight to physical harm or mental degradation in every single case. Apparently, most people who use it can do so gracefully, without injury to themselves or others.

Drinking, we found, can be viewed medically as ingestion of a drug; drunkenness, as overdosing. The misuse of this drug can, directly and indirectly, lead to problems of all sorts—physical, psychological, domestic, social, financial, vocational. Instead of thinking mostly about what drinking did *for* us, we began to see what it does *to* some people.

We have found out that *anybody* who has trouble of any sort related to drinking may have the condition called "alcoholism." This illness strikes without regard for age, creed, sex, intelligence, ethnic background, emotional health, occupation, family situation, strong constitution, eating habits, social or economic status, or general character. It is not a question of how much or how you drink, or when, or why, but of how your drinking affects your life—what happens when you drink.

Before we could recognize the illness in ourselves, we had to unload this tired old myth: It would be a sign of shameful weakness to admit that we couldn't handle the sauce any more (if we ever could).

Weakness? Actually, it takes considerable courage to stare unblinkingly at the hard truth, sparing nothing, without glossing over anything, without excuses, and without kidding ourselves. (It is unseemly to brag, but frankly, many of us think that at kidding ourselves we were world champions.)

The process of recovery from alcoholism also has been clouded with misconceptions. Like millions of others who have watched a person drinking himself or herself to death, we have wondered why the drinker did not use willpower to stop drinking. That is another outdated idea, but it sticks because many of us have been exposed early in life to some model of superwillpower. Maybe there was the family or neighborhood legend of good old Uncle John. Known as a rake and a heller for years, he suddenly gave up wine, women, and song at age 50 and became a model of propriety and rectitude who never touched another drop.

The childish notion that we can do likewise when we get ready is a dangerous delusion. We are not anybody else. We are only ourselves. (We are not Grandpa, who drank a fifth a day until he was 90, either.)

It is now well established that willpower all by itself is about as effective a cure for alcohol addiction as it is for cancer. Our own experience has verified that repeatedly. Most of us tried going it alone, hoping either to control our drinking or to stop, and we had no lasting success in either endeavor. Even so, it wasn't easy to admit we needed help. That, too, looked like a sign of weakness. Yes, we were being taken in by another myth.

But we finally asked ourselves: Wouldn't it be more intelligent to seek out and tap a strength greater than our own than to persist in our futile solo efforts, after they had time and again been proved ineffective? We still don't think it is very smart to keep trying to see in the dark if you can simply switch on a lamp and use its light. We didn't get sober entirely on our own. That isn't the way we learned to stay sober. And the full enjoyment of living sober isn't a one-person job, either.

When we could look, even temporarily, at just a few new ideas different from our old ones, we had already begun to make a sturdy start toward a happy, healthier new life. It happened just that way to thousands and thousands of us who deeply believed it never could.

28 Reading the A.A. message

Human beings, we are told, learn many things best by seeing and touching as well as hearing them; and reading about them reinforces the strength of such learning even further.

There are many good publications on alcoholism, and some not so good. Many of us have also profited by reading in other fields. But A.A. neither endorses nor opposes anybody else's publications. We simply offer our own.

Even drinkers who have never before been much for reading spend hours poring over A.A. material. It is undoubtedly the best way to grasp a broad, firsthand consensus of all A.A. wisdom, instead of just the hearsay of one time and place.

There are seven A.A. books and three booklets in a format similar to this one.

"Alcoholics Anonymous"

This is the basic textbook of A.A. experience.

A.A. as we know it is the outgrowth of this book, which was originally prepared by a hundred or so alcoholics who had learned to stay sober by helping each other. After a few years of sobriety, they recorded what they had done and gave the account this title. Our Fellowship then began to be called by the name "Alcoholics Anonymous."

In this volume, the original A.A. experience is spelled out by those who did it first, then wrote about it. It is the primary source book of all basic A.A. thought for all of us—whether we read and reread it often or seldom. Most members get a copy as soon after coming to A.A. as they can, so they may take the fundamental A.A. ideas directly from the source, not hear of them second- or third-hand.

Members often refer to "Alcoholics Anonymous" as the "Big Book," but not to compare it with any sacred text. Its first printing (in 1939) was on very thick paper, so it came out surprisingly fat and was laughingly dubbed the Big Book.

The first 11, basic chapters were written by Bill W., co-founder of A.A. It also contains many A.A. members' own stories, as written by themselves, and several appendixes of additional matter.

Simply reading the book was enough to sober up some people in A.A.'s early days, when there were only a few A.A. groups in the world. It still works that way for some problem drinkers in isolated parts of the world, or for those who live on seagoing vessels.

Regular readers of the book say that repeated readings reveal many deeper meanings that cannot be grasped at the first hurried glance.

"Twelve Steps and Twelve Traditions"

A.A. fundamentals are discussed at even greater depth in this book, also written by Bill W. (It is sometimes nicknamed "The Twelve and Twelve.") Members who want to study the A.A. program of recovery seriously use it as a text, in conjunction with the Big Book.

Written 13 years after "Alcoholics Anonymous," this smaller volume explains principles of A.A. behavior, both individual and group. The Twelve Steps, guides to individual growth, had been discussed more briefly in the Big Book; the group principles—the Twelve Traditions—became crystallized through trial and error, after the first book was published. They characterize the movement and make it unique—quite unlike other societies.

"Alcoholics Anonymous Comes of Age"

This brief history tells how the Fellowship started, and how it grew for its first 20 years. It recounts the tale of how a small group of courageous, once-hopeless former drunkards—with all the odds against them—finally became securely established as a worldwide movement of acknowledged effectiveness.

"As Bill Sees It"

A reader of Bill W.'s pithiest paragraphs, from his voluminous personal correspondence as well as other writings. A subject index covers topics of interest to any problem drinker.

"Dr. Bob and the Good Oldtimers"

The life story of A.A.'s co-founder is interwoven with recollections of early A.A. in the Midwest, mostly in pioneer members' own words.

"Pass It On"

This biography of A.A.'s co-founder is subtitled "The Story of Bill Wilson and How the A.A. Message Reached The World." It also traces the development of the Fellowship; 39 photographs from A.A.'s history.

"Came to Believe..."

Subtitled "The Spiritual Adventure of A.A. as Experienced by Individual Members," this is a collection of 75 members' versions of "a Power greater than ourselves." They range from orthodox religious interpretations through humanistic and agnostic views.

"Daily Reflections: A Book of Reflections by A.A. Members for A.A. Members"

A.A.s reflect on favorite quotations from A.A. literature. A reading for each day of the year.

"A.A. in Prison: Inmate to Inmate"

A collection of 32 stories, previously printed in the A.A. Grapevine, sharing the experience of men and women who found A.A. while in prison.

Pamphlets

Many leaflets on various aspects of A.A., some of them addressed to special-interest groups, are also published by A.A. World Services, Inc.

They have all been carefully prepared under close supervision by

A.A. representatives from all over the U.S. and Canada, so that they represent the broadest possible consensus of A.A. thinking. It is impossible to understand all the workings of A.A. unless one is well acquainted with all these publications (complete listing on page 90).

In addition, the A.A. General Service Office produces a bimonthly newsletter, *Box 4-5-9*, and several other periodical bulletins, as well as a report on the annual General Service Conference of A.A.

Many A.A. members start and end each day with a quiet moment in which they read a passage of some A.A. literature. Poring over A.A. books and pamphlets represents "a meeting in print" for many members, and the range of A.A. information and inspiration summed up in them cannot be found anywhere else. Any A.A. reading starts a trail of A.A. thinking which leads away from a drink, so many A.A.'s always carry with them some piece of A.A. literature—not just because reading it can help ward off the kind of thinking that leads to drinking, but also because it can afford refreshment and entertainment for the mind at odd moments. A.A. literature not available at an A.A. meeting can be ordered directly by writing to: Box 459, Grand Central Station, New York, NY 10163.

The A.A. Grapevine

Every month, a fresh collection of A.A. thought and humor appears in this magazine. Almost all its articles, graphics, and cartoons are by A.A. members. The writers are not paid, and many illustrations also are contributed free.

It contains thought pieces, illustrated stories, news about A.A., letters from A.A. members around the globe, and inspirational articles (no poems).

Individual subscriptions may be ordered directly by writing to: Box 1980, Grand Central Station, New York, NY 10163. Copies of the current issue are usually available at meetings of A.A. groups.

29 Going to A.A. meetings

Long before this booklet was even thought of, every single idea in it and many more suggestions for living sober were learned and *proved successful* by hundreds of thousands of alcoholics. We did this not just by reading, but also by talking to each other. At first, we mostly listened.

You can easily do the same thing, free, and you don't have to "join" anything.

What we did was simply go to meetings of Alcoholics Anonymous. There are over five million each year, in approximately 150 countries around the globe. And remember, you do not have to become an A.A. member in order to visit some A.A. meetings. If all you want to do is sort of "try out" A.A., you are entirely welcome to attend A.A. meetings as an observer and just listen quietly, without saying a word. You don't need to give your name, or you can give a phony one if you want to. A.A. understands. It doesn't record names of either members or visitors attending its meetings, anyhow. You won't have to sign anything, or answer any questions.

Feel free to ask some, if you wish. But many people prefer just to listen the first few times.

Like practically everyone else who has gone to an A.A. meeting, you'll probably be very surprised the first time. The people you see around you look mostly normal, healthy, reasonably happy, and successful. They do not look like old-fashioned cartoons of drunkards, bums, or fanatic, dried-up teetotalers.

What's more, you'll usually find us quite a friendly bunch, doing a lot of laughing—at ourselves. That is why, if you are hung-over, an A.A. gathering provides a cheerful environment for getting past the hangover and beginning to feel much, much better.

You can be very sure that every A.A. member in that room deeply understands exactly how you feel, because we remember vividly our own hangover miseries, and how it felt the first time we ever went to an A.A. meeting.

If you are shy, kind of a loner—just like many of us—you'll find the A.A. members willing to let you pretty much alone if that is really what you want and it makes you more comfortable.

However, most of us found it much more beneficial to hang around for a bite and a chat after the meeting. Feel free to participate in the socializing, or "eyeball-to-eyeball sharing," just as much, or as little, as you wish.

Different kinds of A.A. meetings

Many A.A. members from all over the U.S. and Canada were asked for ideas for this booklet. Near the top in all their lists is the suggestion that one of the surest ways of avoiding drinking is going to various kinds of A.A. meetings. "That's where we learn all these ideas from each other," one member wrote.

If you want to stay sober, going to *any* A.A. meeting is, of course, safer than going to a bar or a party, or staying at home with a bottle!

Chances for avoiding malaria are best when you stay away from a swamp full of mosquitoes. Just so, chances of not drinking are better at an A.A. meeting than they are in a drinking situation.

In addition, at A.A. meetings there is a kind of momentum toward recovery. Whereas drinking is the object of a cocktail party, sobriety is the common goal aimed for at any A.A. meeting. Here, perhaps more than anywhere else, you are surrounded by people who understand drinking, who appreciate your sobriety, and who can tell you many means of furthering it. Besides, you see many, many examples of successfully recovered, happy, nondrinking alcoholics. That's not what you see in barrooms.

Here are the most popular kinds of A.A. group meetings, and some of the benefits derived from attending them.

Beginners (or newcomers) meetings

These are usually smaller than other meetings, and often precede a larger meeting. They are open to anyone who thinks he or she may possibly have a drinking problem. In some places, these meetings are a series of scheduled discussions or talks about alcoholism, about recovery, and about A.A. itself. In others, the beginners meetings are simply question-and-answer sessions.

A.A.'s who have used these meetings a lot point out that these are excellent places to ask questions, to make new friends, and to begin to feel comfortable in the company of alcoholics, not drinking.

Open meetings (anyone welcome, alcoholic or not)

These are likely to be a little more organized, a little more formal. Usually, two or three members (who have volunteered in advance) in turn tell the group about their alcoholism, what happened, and what their recovery is like.

An A.A. talk of this type does not have to follow any set pattern. Of course, only a tiny handful of A.A. members are trained orators. In fact, even those A.A.'s whose jobs involve professional speaking carefully avoid making speeches at A.A. meetings. Instead, they try to tell their own stories as simply and directly as possible.

What is unmistakable is the almost startling sincerity and honesty you hear. You'll probably be surprised to find yourself laughing a lot, and saying to yourself, "Yes, that's just what it's like!"

One of the big benefits of attending such open meetings is the opportunity to hear a wide, wide variety of actual case histories of alcoholism. You hear the symptoms of the illness described in many vary-ing forms, and that helps you decide whether you have it.

Naturally, each A.A. member's experiences have been different from the others'. It is possible that some time you'll hear someone recall favorite drinks, drinking patterns, and drinking problems (or drinking fun) very much like your own. On the other hand, the incidents in the drinking stories you hear may be quite unlike yours. You will hear peo-ple of many different backgrounds, occupations, and beliefs. Each member speaks *only* for himself (or herself), and voices only his own opinions. No one can speak for all of A.A., and no one has to agree with any sentiments or ideas expressed by any other A.A. member. Diversity of opinion is welcomed and valued in A.A.

But if you listen carefully, you will probably recognize familiar feel-ings, if not familiar events. You will recognize the emotions of the speaker as having been much like your own, even if the life you hear about has been radically different from yours.

In A.A., this is called "identifying with the speaker." It does not mean that the age, the sex, the life-style, the behavior, the pleasures, or the troubles of the speaker are identical to yours. But it does mean that you hear of fears, excitements, worries, and joys which you can empathize with, which you remember feeling at times yourself.

It may surprise you that you will almost never hear an A.A. speaker sound self-pitying about being deprived of alcohol.

Identifying with the speaker's past may not be as important as get-ting an impression of his or her present life. The speaker usually has found, or is reaching for, some contentment, peace of mind, solutions to problems, zest for living, and a kind of health of the spirit which you, too, want. If so, hang around. Those qualities are contagious in A.A.

Besides, the reminders you get of the miseries of active alcoholism can help extinguish any lurking desire to take a drink!

At meetings like this, many A.A. members have heard the very tips on recovery they were looking for. And almost all members leave such a meeting so refreshed and so encouraged in their recovery that the last thing on earth they want is a drink.

Closed discussion meetings (only for alcoholics—or for people who are trying to find out whether they are alcoholics)

Some A.A. groups hold discussion meetings labeled "open," so any-one is welcome to attend. More often, such meetings are described as "closed," for members or prospective members only, so those who at-tend can feel free to discuss any topic that might trouble—or interest—any problem drinker. These are confidential discussions.

A member who has volunteered in advance may lead off the meeting by telling briefly of his or her own alcoholism and recovery. The meeting is then open for general discussion.

Anyone troubled by a particular problem, no matter how painful or embarrassing, may air it at a discussion meeting and hear from others present their experiences at handling the same or a similar problem. And yes, experiences of happiness and joy are shared, too. One surely learns in such discussions that no alcoholic is unique or alone.

It has been said that these meetings are the workshops in which an alcoholic learns how to stay sober. Certainly, one can pick up at discussion meetings a broad range of suggestions for maintaining a happy sobriety.

Step meetings

Many A.A. groups hold weekly meetings at which one of the Twelve Steps of the A.A. program is taken up in turn and forms the basis of the discussion. A.A.'s Twelve Traditions, the Three Legacies of A.A., A.A. slogans, and discussion topics suggested in A.A.'s monthly magazine, the Grapevine, are also used by some groups for this purpose. But other topics are almost never ruled out, especially if someone present feels an urgent need for help with an immediate, pressing personal problem.

In conjunction with the books "Alcoholics Anonymous" and "Twelve Steps and Twelve Traditions," Step meetings afford perhaps the most easily grasped insights into and understanding of the fundamental principles of recovery in A.A. These sessions also furnish a wealth of original interpretations and applications of the basic A.A. program—showing how we can use it, not only to stay sober, but to enrich our lives.

State, regional, national, and international A.A. conventions and conferences

Attended by anywhere from hundreds to more than 20,000 A.A. members, often accompanied by their families, these king-size A.A. gatherings usually are weekend affairs consisting of many kinds of session. The programs often include discussion workshops on varied topics, as well as talks by guest experts on alcoholism, and usually a banquet, a dance, entertainment, and time for other social or recreational activities, all the more highly enjoyed because they are alcoholfree. They show us how much fun we can have sober.

They also give us a chance to meet and learn from A.A.'s who live in other areas. For many members, these occasions become favorite holiday weekends, as well as highly prized, peak experiences in recovery. They provide inspiring memories to cherish on ordinary days, and often see the start of close, lifelong friendships.

Do we have to go to those meetings for the rest of our lives?

Not at all, unless we want to.

Thousands of us seem to enjoy meetings more and more as the sober years go by. So it is a pleasure, not a duty.

We all have to keep on eating, bathing, breathing, brushing our teeth, and the like. And millions of people continue year after year working, reading, going in for sports and other recreation, frequenting social clubs, and performing religious worship. So our continued attendance at A.A. meetings is hardly peculiar, as long as we enjoy them, profit from them, and keep the rest of our lives in balance.

But most of us go to meetings more frequently in the first years of our recovery than we do later. It helps set a solid foundation for a long-term recovery.

Most A.A. groups hold one or two meetings a week (lasting about an hour or an hour and a half). And it is widely believed in A.A. that a new A.A. member fares best by getting into the habit of regularly attending the meetings of at least one group, as well as visiting other groups from time to time. This not only provides a big choice of differing A.A. ideas; it also helps bring into the problem drinker's life a measure of orderliness, which helps combat alcoholism.

We have found it quite important, especially in the beginning, to attend meetings faithfully, no matter what excuses present themselves for staying away.

We need to be as diligent in attending A.A. meetings as we were in drinking. What serious drinker ever let distance, or weather, or illness, or business, or guests, or being broke, or the hour, or anything else keep him or her from that really wanted drink? We cannot let anything keep us from A.A. meetings, either, if we really want to recover.

We have also found that going to meetings is *not* something to be done only when we feel the temptation to drink. We often get more good from the meetings by attending them when we feel fine and haven't so much as thought of drinking. And even a meeting which is not totally, instantly satisfying is better than no meeting at all.

Because of the importance of meetings, many of us keep a list of local meetings with us at all times, and never travel far from home base without taking along one of the A.A. directories, which enable us to find meetings or fellow members almost anywhere on earth.

When serious illness or natural catastrophe makes missing a meeting absolutely unavoidable, we have learned to work out substitutes for the meetings. (It's amazing, though, how often we hear that blizzards in subarctic regions, hurricanes, and even earthquakes have *not* prevented A.A.'s from traveling a hundred miles or more to get to meetings. With a meeting to reach, getting there by canoe, camel, helicopter, jeep, truck, bicycle, or sleigh is as natural to some A.A.'s as using cars, buses, or subways is for the rest of us.)

As a substitute for a meeting, when attendance is impossible, we may call A.A. friends on the telephone or by ham radio; or we may hold a meeting in our minds while reading some A.A. material.

For several hundred isolated A.A. "Loners" (such as armed services personnel far from home), and for several hundred seagoing A.A. "Internationalists," special services are provided free by the General Service Office of A.A. to help them keep in close contact with A.A. They receive bulletins and lists that enable them to communicate with other members (by letter or sometimes tape) between the times they find it possible to go to regular A.A. meetings.

But many of those who are on their own do something even better when they find no A.A. group near enough for them to attend. They start a group.

The money question

Alcoholism is expensive. Although A.A. itself charges no dues or fees whatsoever, we have already paid pretty heavy "dues" to liquor stores and bartenders before we get here. Therefore, many of us arrive at A.A. nearly broke, if not heavily in debt.

The sooner we can become self-supporting, the better, we have found. Creditors are almost always happy to go along with us as long as they see we are really making an honest, regular effort to climb out of the hole, even in tiny installments.

A particular kind of expenditure, however—in addition to food, clothing, and shelter, naturally—has been found extremely valuable in our first sober days. One of us has given his permission to print here his

Investment Counsel

In the first few weeks without a drink
When the wolf is at the door,
And the sheriff's at the window
And you're sleeping on the floor,
And life looks bleak and hopeless
From a monetary angle,
It's time to *spend,* in certain ways,
To solve the awful tangle:
That token or that bus fare
To get you to a meeting,
That dime to use the telephone

For that necessary greeting,
That nickel for "expenses"
That makes you feel you matter,
That dollar for the coffee shop
For after-meeting chatter.
All these are wise investments
For the neophyte to make.
This "bread," when cast upon the waters,
Always comes back cake.

30 Trying the Twelve Steps

"When all else fails," said the old country doctor, "follow directions."

We have not talked about the Twelve Steps offered by A.A. as a program of recovery from alcoholism, and they are not going to be listed or explained here, because anyone curious about them can find them elsewhere. Their origin is striking, however.

In 1935, two men met in Akron, Ohio. Both of them were then considered hopeless drunkards, which seemed shameful to those who had known them. One had been a Wall Street hot shot; the other, a noted surgeon; but both had drunk themselves almost to death. Each had tried many "cures" and been hospitalized over and over. It looked certain, even to them, that they were beyond help.

Almost accidentally, in getting to know each other, they stumbled onto an astonishing fact: When each of them tried to help the other, the result was sobriety. They took the idea to an alcoholic lawyer confined to a hospital bed, and he, too, decided to try it.

The three then kept on, each in his individual life, trying to help one alcoholic after another. If the people they tried to help sometimes did not want their aid, they nevertheless knew the effort was worthwhile, because, in each case, the would-be helper stayed sober even if the "patient" kept on drinking.

Persisting at this avocation for their own benefit, this nameless little band of ex-drunks suddenly realized in 1937 that 20 of them were sober! They cannot be blamed for thinking a miracle had happened.

They agreed they ought to write a record of what had happened, so their experience could be widely distributed. But, as you can imagine, they ran into real difficulty in reaching agreement on what precisely had taken place. It wasn't until 1939 that they were able to publish an account they could all subscribe to. By then, they numbered about 100.

They wrote that the pathway to recovery they had followed up to then consisted of twelve steps, and they believed anyone who followed that pathway would reach the same destination.

Their number has grown to more than two million. And they are virtually unanimous in their conviction: "Practical experience shows that nothing will so much insure immunity from drinking as intensive work with other alcoholics. It works when other activities fail."

Many of us had long been booze-fighters. Time after time, we had stopped drinking and tried to stay stopped, only to return to drinking sooner or later and find ourselves in increasing trouble. But those Twelve Steps of A.A. mark our road to recovery. Now, we do not have to fight any more. And our path is open to all comers.

Hundreds of us had only a vague idea of what A.A. was before we actually came to this Fellowship. Now, we sometimes think there is more misinformation than truth about A.A. floating around. So if you have not looked into A.A. firsthand, we can imagine some of the distorted, false impressions you may have picked up, since we had so many of them ourselves.

Happily, you need not be misled by such misrepresentations and rumors, because it is perfectly easy to see and hear the real A.A. for yourself. A.A. publications (see page 70) and any nearby A.A. office or meeting (see your local telephone directory) are original sources of facts which surprised many of us a whale of a lot. You need not take any second-hand opinions, because you can get the straight dope, free, and make up your own mind.

Really getting a fair picture of A.A. may be one instance in which willpower can be put to very good use. We know for sure that alcoholics do have tremendous willpower. Consider the ways we could manage to get a drink in defiance of all visible possibilities. Merely to get up some mornings—with a rusting cast-iron stomach, all your teeth wearing tiny sweaters, and each hair electrified—takes willpower many nondrinkers rarely dream of. Once you've gotten up with your head, on those certain mornings, the ability to carry it all through the day is further evidence of fabulous strength of will. Oh yes, *real* drinkers have *real* willpower.

The trick we learned was to put that will to work for our health, and to *make* ourselves explore recovery ideas at great depth, even though it sometimes might have seemed like drudgery.

It may help if you try to remember that A.A. members are not eager to question you. We may not even seem to be listening to you much, but spend more time laying on you the unvarnished facts of our own illness. We are in pursuit of recovery, you know, so we talk to you very much for our own benefit. We want to help you, all right, but only if you want us to.

It may be that problem drinking is, indeed, as some psychological experts say, an ailment characterized especially by egocentricity. Not all alcoholics are egotistical, although many of us have learned to see that tendency in ourselves. Others of us felt inferior most of the time; we felt equal or superior to other people only when drinking.

No matter which type we were, we realize now that we were excessively self-centered, chiefly concerned about *our* feelings, *our* problems, other people's reactions to *us*, and *our* own past and future. Therefore, trying to get into communication with and to help other people is a recovery measure for us, because it helps take us out of ourselves. Trying to heal ourselves by helping others works, even when it is an insincere gesture. Try it some time.

If you really listen to (not just hear) what is being said, you may find the person talking has quietly slipped inside your head and seems to be describing the landscape there—the shifting shapes of nameless fears, the color and chill of impending doom—if not the actual events and words stored in your brain.

And whether this happens or not, you will almost surely have a good laugh or two in the company of A.A.'s, and you'll probably pick up a couple of ideas on living sober. If you want to use them, that is up to you.

Whatever you decide to do, remember that making these ideas available is one of the steps toward recovery for us.

31 Finding your own way

We hope this booklet has made it eminently clear that we don't consider drinking a frivolous subject. Alcoholism deserves and gets dead serious attention from us. We do not find jokes told at the expense of sick problem drinkers funny, except those we tell on ourselves from our vantage point of sobriety. We aren't amused when someone teasingly threatens to get drunk. That's like teasing about Russian roulette.

In spite of our serious attitude toward alcoholism, you will find we can usually talk with humor and detachment about our past and our recovery. This is a healthy approach, we think. Certainly, it does not weaken our resolve to get and stay well.

Most of us have seen death close up. We have known the kind of suffering that wrenches the bones. But we also have known the sort of hope that makes the heart sing. And we hope this booklet has conveyed to you more encouragement than pain. If you are a problem drinker, you already know enough about pain and loneliness. We'd like you to find some of the peace and joy we have found in meeting the reality of life's ups and downs with a clear head and a steady heart.

No doubt, we have made just a bare beginning in the business of living sober. Time and again, we learn additional ideas that can help.

As you stay sober, you are sure to think of new ideas not recorded here. We hope so. We also hope that when you do come up with fresh ideas on this subject, you will pass them on. Please do share. (You'll recall that the act of sharing can itself be helpful to you.) The more experience we can all pool, the more problem drinkers can be helped.

Some of us go back to drinking a time or so before we get a real foothold on sobriety. If that happens to you, don't despair. Many of us have done this and have finally come through to successful sobriety. Try to remember that alcoholism is an extremely serious human condition, and that relapses are as possible in this ailment as in others. Recovery can still follow.

Even after setbacks, if you continue to want to get well, and remain willing to try new approaches, our experience convinces us that you have embarked with hundreds of thousands of companions on the path of a happy, healthy destiny. We hope we see you among us in person.

But whatever track you travel, along with us or on your own, you go with our strongest good wishes.

Appendix*

A report from a group of physicians in A.A.

Because this subject is one which goes deeply into the field of medicine, a group of physicians who are members of A.A. was asked to help prepare this material.

The experience of some A.A. members reveals that drug misuse can threaten the achievement and maintenance of sobriety.

Yet some A.A. members must take prescribed medication in order to treat certain serious medical problems.

Experience has shown that this problem can be minimized if the following suggestions are carefully heeded:

1 Remember that as a recovering alcoholic your automatic response will be to turn to chemical relief for uncomfortable feelings and to take more than the usual, prescribed amount. Look for nonchemical solutions for the aches and discomforts of everyday living.

2 Remember that the best safeguard against drug-related relapse is an active participation in the A.A. program of recovery.

3 No A.A. member plays doctor.

4 Be completely honest with yourself and your physician regarding use of medication.

5 If in doubt, consult a physician with demonstrated experience in the treatment of alcoholism.

6 Be frank about your alcoholism with any physician or dentist you consult. Such confidence will be respected and is most helpful to the doctor.

7 Inform the physician at once if you experience side effects from prescribed drugs.

---

* From the Conference-approved pamphlet "The A.A. Member—Medications and Other Drugs."

8 Consider consulting another doctor if a personal physician refuses or fails to recognize the peculiar susceptibility of alcoholics to sedatives, tranquilizers, and stimulants.

9 Give your doctor copies of this pamphlet [The A.A. Member—Medications and Other Drugs].

However, some alcoholics require medication...

At the same time that we recognize this dangerous tendency to readdiction, we also recognize that alcoholics are *not immune* to other diseases. Some of us have had to cope with depressions that can be suicidal; schizophrenia that sometimes requires hospitalization; manic depression; and other mental and biological illnesses. Also among us are epileptics, members with heart trouble, cancer, allergies, hypertension, and many other serious physical conditions.

Because of the difficulties that many alcoholics have with drugs, some members have taken the position that no one in A.A. should take any medication. While this position has undoubtedly prevented relapses for some, it has meant disaster for others.

A.A. members and many of their physicians have described situations in which depressed patients have been told by A.A.s to throw away the pills, only to have depression return with all its difficulties, sometimes resulting in suicide. We have heard, too, from schizophrenics, manic depressives, epileptics, and others requiring medication that well-meaning A.A. friends often discourage them from taking prescribed medication. Unfortunately, by following a layman's advice, the sufferers find that their conditions can return with all their previous intensity. On top of that, they feel guilty because they are convinced that "A.A. is against pills."

It becomes clear that just as it is wrong to enable or support any alcoholic to become readdicted to any drug, it's equally wrong to deprive any alcoholic of medication which can alleviate or control other disabling physical and/or emotional problems.

A.A. Pamphlets

44 QUESTIONS
A.A. TRADITION—HOW IT DEVELOPED
MEMBERS OF THE CLERGY ASK ABOUT A.A.
THREE TALKS TO MEDICAL SOCIETIES BY BILL W.
ALCOHOLICS ANONYMOUS AS A RESOURCE FOR
THE HEALTH CARE PROFESSIONAL
A.A. IN YOUR COMMUNITY
IS A.A. FOR YOU?
IS A.A. FOR ME?
THIS IS A.A.
IS THERE AN ALCOHOLIC IN THE WORKPLACE?
DO YOU THINK YOU'RE DIFFERENT?
QUESTIONS AND ANSWERS ON SPONSORSHIP
A.A. FOR THE WOMAN
A.A. FOR THE NATIVE NORTH AMERICAN
A.A. AND THE GAY/LESBIAN ALCOHOLIC
TIME TO START LIVING *(A pamphlet for the older alcoholic,*
also available in large print)
THE JACK ALEXANDER ARTICLE
LETTER TO A WOMAN ALCOHOLIC
YOUNG PEOPLE AND A.A.
A.A. AND THE ARMED SERVICES
THE A.A. MEMBER—MEDICATIONS AND OTHER DRUGS
IS THERE AN ALCOHOLIC IN YOUR LIFE?
INSIDE A.A.
THE A.A. GROUP
G.S.R.
MEMO TO AN INMATE
THE TWELVE CONCEPTS ILLUSTRATED
THE TWELVE TRADITIONS ILLUSTRATED
LET'S BE FRIENDLY WITH OUR FRIENDS
HOW A.A. MEMBERS COOPERATE
A.A. IN CORRECTIONAL FACILITIES
A MESSAGE TO CORRECTIONAL PROFESSIONALS
A.A. IN TREATMENT FACILITIES
BRIDGING THE GAP
IF YOU ARE A PROFESSIONAL
A.A. MEMBERSHIP SURVEY
A MEMBER'S-EYE VIEW OF ALCOHOLICS ANONYMOUS
PROBLEMS OTHER THAN ALCOHOL
UNDERSTANDING ANONYMITY
THE CO-FOUNDERS OF ALCOHOLICS ANONYMOUS
SPEAKING AT NON-A.A. MEETINGS
A BRIEF GUIDE TO A.A.
A NEWCOMER ASKS
WHAT HAPPENED TO JOE; IT HAPPENED TO ALICE
(Two full-color, comic-book style pamphlets)
TOO YOUNG? *(A cartoon pamphlet for teenagers)*
IT SURE BEATS SITTING IN A CELL
(An Illustrated pamphlet for inmates)

Complete order forms from A.A. General Service Office:
Box 459, Grand Central Station, New York, NY 10163